CAMBRIDGE LIBRARY COLLECTION

Books of enduring scholarly value

History of Oceania

This series focuses on Australia, New Zealand and the Pacific region from the arrival of European seafarers and missionaries to the early twentieth century. Contemporary accounts document the gradual development of the European settlements from penal colonies and whaling stations to thriving communities of farmers, miners and traders with fully-fledged administrative and legal systems. Particularly noteworthy are the descriptions of the indigenous peoples of the various islands, their customs, and their differing interactions with the European settlers.

A Narrative of the Expedition to Botany Bay

In May 1787, eleven ships left England with more than seven hundred convicts on board, along with orders to establish a penal colony at Botany Bay, New South Wales. Watkin Tench (*c*.1758–1833) was a crew member on one of the ships of this First Fleet, the *Charlotte*, and he recalls the voyage and early days of the settlement in this vivid and engaging account, first published in 1789. The first half of the work retraces the route of the six-month journey, which took the fleet to Brazil and the Cape of Good Hope. The later chapters recount the landing at Botany Bay in January 1788, the establishment of a colony at nearby Port Jackson and observations about the natural world in this new settlement. Tench also discusses the initial interaction with the Aboriginal people, making this work an important source for scholars of British colonialism and Australian history.

Cambridge University Press has long been a pioneer in the reissuing of out-of-print titles from its own backlist, producing digital reprints of books that are still sought after by scholars and students but could not be reprinted economically using traditional technology. The Cambridge Library Collection extends this activity to a wider range of books which are still of importance to researchers and professionals, either for the source material they contain, or as landmarks in the history of their academic discipline.

Drawing from the world-renowned collections in the Cambridge University Library and other partner libraries, and guided by the advice of experts in each subject area, Cambridge University Press is using state-of-the-art scanning machines in its own Printing House to capture the content of each book selected for inclusion. The files are processed to give a consistently clear, crisp image, and the books finished to the high quality standard for which the Press is recognised around the world. The latest print-on-demand technology ensures that the books will remain available indefinitely, and that orders for single or multiple copies can quickly be supplied.

The Cambridge Library Collection brings back to life books of enduring scholarly value (including out-of-copyright works originally issued by other publishers) across a wide range of disciplines in the humanities and social sciences and in science and technology.

A Narrative of the Expedition to Botany Bay

With an Account of New South Wales, Its Productions, Inhabitants, etc.

Watkin Tench

CAMBRIDGE
UNIVERSITY PRESS

University Printing House, Cambridge, CB2 8BS, United Kingdom

Published in the United States of America by Cambridge University Press, New York

Cambridge University Press is part of the University of Cambridge.
It furthers the University's mission by disseminating knowledge in the pursuit of education, learning and research at the highest international levels of excellence.

www.cambridge.org
Information on this title: www.cambridge.org/9781108061681

This edition first published 1789
This digitally printed version 2013

ISBN 978-1-108-06168-1 Paperback

A NARRATIVE OF THE EXPEDITION TO BOTANY BAY.

A NARRATIVE OF THE EXPEDITION TO BOTANY BAY;

WITH AN ACCOUNT OF

NEW SOUTH WALES,
ITS PRODUCTIONS, INHABITANTS, &c.

TO WHICH IS SUBJOINED,

A LIST of the CIVIL and MILITARY ESTABLISHMENTS at PORT JACKSON.

BY CAPTAIN WATKIN TENCH,
OF THE MARINES.

LONDON:

PRINTED FOR J. DEBRETT, OPPOSITE
BURLINGTON-HOUSE, PICCADILLY.

1789.

INTRODUCTION,

IN offering this little tract to the public, it is equally the writer's wiſh to conduce to their amuſement and information.

The expedition on which he is engaged has excited much curioſity, and given birth to many ſpeculations, reſpecting the conſequences to ariſe from it. While men continue to think freely, they will judge variouſly. Some have been ſanguine enough to foreſee the moſt beneficial effects to the Parent State, from the Colony we are endeavouring to eſtabliſh; and ſome have not been wanting to pronounce the ſcheme big with folly, impolicy, and ruin. Which of theſe predictions will be completed, I leave to the deciſion of the public. I cannot, how-

however, diſmiſs the ſubject without expreſſing a hope, that the candid and liberal of each opinion, induced by the humane and benevolent intention in which it originated, will unite in waiting the reſult of a fair trial to an experiment, no leſs new in its deſign, than difficult in its execution.

As this publication enters the world with the name of the author, candour will, he truſts, induce its readers to believe, that no conſideration could weigh with him in an endeavour to miſlead them. Facts are related ſimply as they happened, and when opinions are hazarded, they are ſuch as, he hopes, patient inquiry, and deliberate deciſion, will be found to have authoriſed. For the moſt part he has ſpoken from actual obſervation; and in thoſe places where the relations of others have been unavoidably adopted, he has been careful to ſearch for the truth, and repreſs that ſpirit of exaggeration which is almoſt ever the effect of novelty on ignorance.

The

The nautical part of the work, is comprized in as few pages as poſſible. By the profeſſional part of my readers this will be deemed judicious; and the reſt will not, I believe, be diſſatisfied at its brevity. I beg leave, however, to ſay of the aſtronomical calculations, that they may be depended on with the greateſt degree of ſecurity, as they were communicated by an officer, who was furniſhed with inſtruments, and commiſſioned by the Board of Longitude, to make obſervations during the voyage, and in the ſouthern hemiſphere.

An unpractiſed writer is generally anxious to beſpeak public attention, and to ſolicit public indulgence. Except on profeſſional ſubjects, military men are, perhaps, too fearful of critical cenſure. For the preſent narrative no other apology is attempted, than the intentions of its author, who has endeavoured not only to ſatisfy preſent curioſity, but to point out to future adventurers, the favourable, as well as adverſe circumſtances which will attend their ſettling here. The candid, it is hoped, will overlook the inaccuracies of this imperfect ſketch, drawn amidſt the complicated duties of the ſervice in which the Author is engaged, and make due allowance for the want of opportunity of gaining more extenſive information.

WATKIN TENCH,
Capt. of the Marines.

Sydney Cove, Port Jackſon,
New South Wales,
July 10, 1788.

THE

CONTENTS.

CHAP. I.

CONTENTS.

XIII. *Tran-*

CONTENTS.

EXPEDITION

TO

BOTANY BAY.

CHAP. I.

From the Embarkation of the Convicts to the Departure of the Ships from England.

THE marines and convicts having been previoufly embarked in the river, at Portfmouth, and Plymouth, the whole fleet deftined for the expedition rendezvoufed at the Mother Bank, on the 16th of March 1787, and remained there until the 13th of May following. In this period, excepting a flight appearance of contagion in one of

the

the tranſports, the ſhips were univerſally healthy, and the priſoners in high ſpirits. Few complaints or lamentations were to be heard among them, and an ardent wiſh for the hour of departure ſeemed generally to prevail.

As the reputation, equally with the ſafety of the officers and ſoldiers appointed to guard the convicts, conſiſted in maintaining due ſubordination, an opportunity was taken, immediately on their being embarked, to convince them, in the moſt pointed terms, that any attempt on their ſide, either to conteſt the command, or to force their eſcape, ſhould be puniſhed with inſtant death; orders to this effect were given to the centinels in their preſence; happily, however, for all parties, there occurred not any inſtance in which there was occaſion to have recourſe to ſo deſperate a meaſure; the behaviour of the convicts being in general humble, ſubmiſſive, and regular: indeed, I ſhould feel myſelf wanting in juſtice to thoſe unfortunate men, were I not to bear this

public

public teſtimony of the ſobriety and decency of their conduct.

Unpleaſant as a ſtate of inactivity and delay for many weeks appeared to us, it was not without its advantages; for by means of it we were enabled to eſtabliſh neceſſary regulations among the convicts, and to adopt ſuch a ſyſtem of defence, as left us little to apprehend for our own ſecurity, in caſe a ſpirit of madneſs and deſperation had hurried them on to attempt our deſtruction.

Among many other troubleſome parts of duty which the ſervice we were engaged on required, the inſpection of all letters brought to, or ſent from the ſhips, was not one of the leaſt tireſome and diſagreeable. The number and contents of thoſe in the veſſel I was embarked in, frequently ſurpriſed me very much; they varied according to the diſpoſitions of the writers: but their conſtant language was, an apprehenſion of the impracticability of returning home, the dread of a ſickly paſſage, and the fearful proſpect of a diſtant and barbarous country. But this apparent despondency proceeded in few instances from sentiment. With too many it was, doubtless, an artifice to awaken compassion, and call forth relief; the correspondence invariably ending in a petition for money and tobacco. Perhaps a want of the latter, which is considered a great luxury by its admirers among the lower classes of life, might be the more severely felt, from their being debarred in all cases whatever, sickness excepted, the use of spirituous liquors.

It may be thought proper for me to mention, that during our stay at the Mother Bank, the soldiers and convicts were indiscriminately served with fresh beef. The former, in addition, had the usual quantity of beer allowed in the navy, and were at what is called full allowance of all species of provisions; the latter, at two thirds only.

CHAP. II.

From the Departure to the Arrival of the Fleet at Teneriffe.

May 1787.

GOVERNOR Phillip having at length reached Portſmouth, and all things deemed neceſſary for the expedition being put on board, at daylight on the morning of the 13th, the ſignal to weigh anchor was made in the Commanding Officer's ſhip the Sirius. Before ſix o'clock the whole fleet were under ſail, and, the weather being fine and wind eaſterly, proceeded through the Needles with a freſh leading breeze. In addition to our little armament, the Hyena frigate was ordered to accompany us a certain diſtance to the weſtward, by which means our number was increaſed to twelve ſail: His Majeſty's ſhips Sirius, Hyena, and Supply, three Victuallers with two years ſtores and proviſions on board for the Settlement, and ſix Tranſports, with troops

troops and convicts. In the tranſports were embarked four captains, twelve ſubalterns, twenty-four ſerjeants and corporals, eight drummers, and one hundred and ſixty private marines, making the whole of the military force, including the Major Commandant and Staff on board the Sirius, to conſiſt of two hundred and twelve perſons, of whom two hundred and ten were volunteers. The number of convicts was five hundred and ſixty-five men, one hundred and ninety-two women, and eighteen children; the major part of the priſoners were mechanics and huſbandmen, ſelected on purpoſe by order of Government.

By ten o'clock we had got clear of the Iſle of Wight, at which time, having very little pleaſure in converſing with my own thoughts, I ſtrolled down among the convicts, to obſerve their ſentiments at this juncture. A very few excepted, their countenances indicated a high degree of ſatisfaction, though in ſome, the pang of being ſevered, perhaps for ever, from their native land,

land, could not be wholly ſuppreſſed; in general, marks of diſtreſs were more perceptible among the men than the women; for I recollect to have ſeen but one of thoſe affected on the occaſion, " Some natural " tears ſhe dropp'd, but wip'd them ſoon " After this the accent of ſorrow was no longer heard; more genial ſkies and change of ſcene baniſhed repining and diſcontent, and introduced in their ſtead cheerfulneſs and acquieſcence in a lot, now not to be altered.

To add to the good diſpoſition which was beginning to manifeſt itſelf, on the morning of the 20th, in conſequence of ſome favorable repreſentations made by the officers commanding detachments, they were hailed and told from the Sirius, that in thoſe caſes where they judged it proper, they were at liberty to releaſe the convicts from the fetters in which they had been hitherto confined. In complying with theſe directions, I had great pleaſure in being able to extend this humane order to the whole of thoſe under my charge, without a ſingle excep-

 tion.

tion. It is hardly neceſſary for me to ſay, that the precaution of ironing the convicts at any time reached to the men only.

In the evening of the ſame day, the Hyena left us for England, which afforded an early opportunity of writing to our friends, and eaſing their apprehenſions by a communication of the favourable accounts it was in our power to ſend them.

From this time to the day of our making the land, little occurred worthy of remark. I cannot, however, help noticing the propriety of employing the marines on a ſervice which requires activity and exertion at ſea, in preference to other troops. Had a regiment recruited ſince the war been ſent out, ſea-ſickneſs would have incapacitated half the men from performing the duties immediately and indiſpenſably neceſſary; whereas the marines, from being accuſtomed to ſerve on board ſhip, accommodated themſelves with eaſe to every exigency, and ſurmounted every difficulty.

At daybreak, on the morning of the 30th of May we ſaw the rocks named the Deſerters, which lie off the ſouth-eaſt end of Madeira; and found the ſouth-eaſt extremity of the moſt ſoutherly of them, to be in the latitude of 32° 28′ north, longitude 16° 17½′ weſt of Greenwich. The following day we ſaw the Salvages, a cluſter of rocks which are placed between the Madeiras and Canary Iſlands, and determined the latitude of the middle of the Great Salvage to be 30° 12′ north, and the longitude of its eaſtern ſide to be 15° 39′ weſt. It is no leſs extraordinary than unpardonable, that in ſome very modern charts of the Atlantic, publiſhed in London, the Salvages are totally omitted.

We made the iſland of Teneriffe on the 3d of June, and in the evening anchored in the road of Santa Cruz, after an excellent paſſage of three weeks from the day we left England.

CHAP. III.

From the Fleet's Arrival at Teneriffe, *to its Departure for* Rio de Janeiro, *in the* Brazils.

THERE is little to pleaſe a traveller at Teneriffe. He has heard wonders of its celebrated Peake, but he may remain for weeks together at the town of Santa Cruz without having a glimpſe of it, and when its cloud-topped head emerges, the chance is, that he feels diſappointed, for, from the point of view in which he ſees it, the neighbouring mountains leſſen its effect very conſiderably. Excepting the Peake, the eye receives little pleaſure from the general face of the country, which is ſterile and uninviting to the laſt degree. The town, however, from its cheerful white appearance, contraſted with the dreary browneſs of the back ground, makes not an unpleaſing *coup d'œil.* It is neither irregular in its plan, nor deſpicable in its ſtyle of building; and the churches

churches and religious houſes are numerous, ſumptuous, and highly ornamented.

The morning of our arrival, as many officers as could be ſpared from the different ſhips were introduced to the Marquis de Brancifort, Governor of the Canary Iſlands, whoſe reception was highly flattering and polite. His Excellency is a Sicilian by birth, and is moſt deſervedly popular in his government. He prefers reſiding at Teneriffe, for the conveniency of frequent communication with Europe, to the Grand Canary, which is properly the ſeat of power; and though not long fixed here, has already found means to eſtabliſh a manufactory in cotton, ſilk, and thread, under excellent regulations, which employs more than ſixty perſons, and is of infinite ſervice to the common people. During our ſhort ſtay we had every day ſome freſh proof of his Excellency's eſteem and attention, and had the honour of dining with him, in a ſtyle of equal elegance and ſplendor. At this entertainment the profuſion of ices which appeared in the deſert was ſurpriſing, conſiderſidering that we were enjoying them under a ſun nearly vertical. But it ſeems the caverns of the Peake, very far below its ſummit, afford, at all ſeaſons, ice in abundance.

The reſtleſs importunity of the beggars, and the immodeſty of the loweſt claſs of women, are highly diſguſting. From the number of his countrymen to be found, an Engliſhman is at no loſs for ſociety. In the mercantile houſes eſtabliſhed here, it is from gentlemen of this deſcription that any information is derived, for the taciturnity of the Spaniärds is not to be overcome in a ſhort acquaintance, eſpecially by Engliſhmen, whoſe reſerve falls little ſhort of their own. The inland country is deſcribed as fertile, and highly romantic; and the environs of the ſmall town of Laguza mentioned as particularly pleaſant. Some of our officers who made an excurſion to it confirmed the account amply.

It ſhould ſeem that the power of the Church, which has been ſo long on the decline

cline in Europe, is at length beginning to be ſhaken in the colonies of the Catholic powers: ſome recent inſtances which have taken place at Teneriffe evince it very fully. Were not a ſtranger, however, to be apprized of this, he would hardly draw the concluſion from his own obſervations. The Biſhop of theſe iſlands, which conjunctively form a See, reſides on the Grand Canary. He is repreſented as a man in years, and of a character as amiable as exalted, extremely beloved both by foreigners and thoſe of his own church. The biſhopric is valued at ten thouſand pounds per annum; the government at ſomewhat leſs than two.

In ſpite of every precaution, while we laid at anchor in the road, a convict had the addreſs, one night, to ſecrete himſelf on the deck, when the reſt were turned below; and after remaining quiet ſome hours, let himſelf down over the bow of the ſhip, and floated to a boat that laid aſtern, into which he got, and cutting her adrift, ſuffered himſelf to be carried away by the current, until at a ſufficient diſtance to be out of hearing, when he rowed off. This elopement was not diſcovered till ſome hours after, when a ſearch being made, and boats ſent to the different parts of the iſland, he was diſcovered in a ſmall cove, to which he had fled for refuge. On being queſtioned, it appeared he had endeavoured to get himſelf received on board a Dutch Eaſt Indiaman in the road, but being rejected there, he reſolved on croſſing over to the Grand Canary, which is at the diſtance of ten leagues, and when detected, was recruiting his ſtrength in order to make the attempt. At the ſame time that the boats of the fleet were ſent on this purſuit, information was given to the Spaniſh Governor of what had happened, who immediately detached parties every way in order to apprehend the delinquent.

Having remained a week at Teneriffe, and in that time completed our ſtock of water, and taken on board wine, &c. early on the morning of the 10th of June we weighed anchor, and ſtood out to ſea with a light eaſterly breeze. The ſhortneſs of our ſtay, and the conſequent hurry, prevented our increaſing much

much any previous knowledge we might have had of the place. For the information of thoſe who may follow us on this ſervice, it may not, however, be amiſs to ſtate the little that will be found of uſe to them.

The markets afford freſh meat, though it is neither plentiful nor good. Fiſh is ſcarce, but poultry may be procured in almoſt any quantity, at as cheap a rate as in the Engliſh ſea-ports. Vegetables do not abound, except pumpkins and onions, of which I adviſe all ſhips to lay in a large ſtock. Milch goats are bought for a trifle, and eaſily procured. Grapes cannot be ſcarce in their ſeaſon, but when we were here, except figs and excellent mulberries, no fruit was to be procured. Dry wines, as the merchants term them, are ſold from ten to fifteen pounds a pipe; for the latter price the very beſt, called the London Particular, may be bought: ſweet wines are conſiderably dearer. Brandy is alſo a cheap article. I would not adviſe the voyager to depend on this place for either his hogs or ſheep. And he will do well to ſupply himſelf with dollars before he quits England, to expend in the different ports he may happen to touch at. Should he, however, have neglected this precaution, let him remember when he discounts bills, or exchanges English money here, not to receive his returns in quarter dollars, which will be tendered to him, but altogether in whole ones, as he will find the latter turn to better account than the former, both at Rio de Janeiro and the Cape of Good Hope.

The latitude of the town of Santa Cruz is 28° 27½′ north, the longitude 16° 17½′ west of Greenwich.

CHAP.

CHAP. IV.

The Paſſage from Teneriffe *to* Rio de Janeiro, *in the* Brazils.

IN ſailing from Teneriffe to the ſouth-eaſt, the various and picturesque appearances of the Peake are beautiful to the higheſt degree. The ſtupendous height, which before was loſt on the traveller, now ſtrikes him with awe and admiration, the whole iſland appearing one vaſt mountain with a pyramidal top. As we proceeded with light winds, at an eaſy rate, we ſaw it diſtinctly for three days after our departure, and ſhould have continued to ſee it longer, had not the hazineſs of the atmoſphere interrupted our view. The good people of Santa Cruz tell ſome ſtories of the wonderful extent of ſpace to be ſeen from the ſummit of it, that would not diſgrace the memoirs of the ever-memorable Baron Munchauſen.

On the 18th of June we saw the most northerly of the Cape de Verd Islands, at which time the Commodore gave the fleet to understand, by signal, that his intention was to touch at some of them. The following day we made St. Jago, and stood in to gain an anchorage in Port Praya Bay. But the baffling winds and lee current rendering it a matter of doubt whether or not the ships would be able to fetch, the signal for anchoring was hauled down, and the fleet bore up before the wind. In passing along them we were enabled to ascertain the south end of the Isle of Sal to be in 16° 40′ north latitude, and 23° 5′ west longitude. The south end of Bonavista to be in 15° 57′ north, 23° 8′ west. The south end of the Isle of May in 15° 11′ north, 23° 26′ west; and the longitude of the fort, in the town of Port Praya, to be 23° 36½′ west of Greenwich.

By this time the weather, from the sun being so far advanced in the northern tropic, was become intolerably hot, which, joined to the heavy rains that soon after came on, made us very apprehensive for the health of the fleet. Contrary, however, to expectation, the number of ſick in the ſhip I was embarked on was ſurpriſingly ſmall, and the reſt of the fleet were nearly as healthy. Frequent exploſions of gunpowder, lighting fires between decks, and a liberal uſe of that admirable antiſeptic, oil of tar, were the preventives we made uſe of againſt impure air; and above all things we were careful to keep the mens' bedding and wearing apparel dry. As we advanced towards the Line the weather grew gradually better and more pleaſant. On the 14th of July we paſſed the Equator, at which time the atmoſphere was as ſerene, and the temperature of the air not hotter than in a bright ſummer day in England. From this period, until our arrival on the American coaſt, the heats, the calms, and the rains by which we had been ſo much incommoded, were ſucceeded by a ſeries of weather as delightful as it was unlooked for. At three o'clock in the afternoon of the 2d of Auguſt, the Supply, which had been previouſly ſent a-head on purpoſe, made the ſignal for ſeeing the land, which was viſible to the whole fleet before sunset, and proved to be Cape Frio, in latitude 23° 5′ south, longitude 41° 40¼′ west.

Owing to light airs we did not get a-breast of the city of St. Sebastian, in the harbour of Rio de Janeiro, until the 7th of the month, when we anchored about three quarters of a mile from the shore.

CHAP.

CHAP. V.

From the Arrival of the Fleet at Rio de Janeiro, *till its Departure for the* Cape of Good Hope, *with ſome Remarks on the* Brazils.

August, 1787.

BRAZIL is a country very imperfectly known in Europe. The Portugueze, from political motives, have been ſparing in their accounts of it. Whence our deſcriptions of it, in the geographical publications in England are drawn, I know not: that they are miſerably erroneous and defective, is certain.

The city of St. Sebaſtian ſtands on the weſt ſide of the harbour, in a low unhealthy ſituation, ſurrounded on all ſides by hills, which ſtop the free circulation of air, and ſubject its inhabitants to intermittents and putrid diſeaſes. It is of conſiderable extent: Mr. Cook makes it as large as Liverpool; but Liverpool, in 1767, when Mr. Cook wrote,

wrote, was not two-thirds of its preſent ſize. Perhaps it equals Cheſter, or Exeter, in the ſhare of ground it occupies, and is infinitely more populous than either of them. The ſtreets interſect each other at right angles, are tolerably well built, and excellently paved, abounding with ſhops of every kind, in which the wants of a ſtranger, if money is not one of them, can hardly remain unſatisfied. About the centre of the city, and at a little diſtance from the beach, the Palace of the Vice-roy ſtands, a long, low building, nowiſe remarkable in its exterior appearance; though within are ſome ſpacious and hand-ſome apartments. The churches and con-vents are numerous, and richly decorated; hardly a night paſſes without ſome of the latter being illuminated, in honour of their patron ſaints, which has a very brilliant ef-fect when viewed from the water, and was at firſt miſtaken by us for public rejoicings. At the corner of almoſt every ſtreet ſtands a little image of the Virgin, ſtuck round with lights in an evening, before which paſſengers frequently ſtop to pray and ſing

very

very loudly. Indeed, the height to which religious zeal is carried in this place, cannot fail of creating aſtoniſhment in a ſtranger. The greateſt part of the inhabitants ſeem to have no other occupation, than that of paying viſits and going to church, at which times you ſee them ſally forth richly dreſſed, en chapeau bras, with the appendages of a bag for the hair, and a ſmall ſword: even boys of ſix years old are ſeen parading about, furniſhed with theſe indiſpenſable requiſites. Except when at their devotions, it is not eaſy to get a ſight of the women, and when obtained, the compariſons drawn by a traveller, lately arrived from England, are little flattering to Portugueze beauty. In juſtice, however, to the ladies of St. Sebaſtian, I muſt obſerve, that the cuſtom of throwing noſegays at ſtrangers, for the purpoſe of bringing on an aſſignation, which Doctor Solander, and another gentleman of Mr. Cook's ſhip met with when here, was never ſeen by any of us in a ſingle inſtance. We were ſo deplorably unfortunate as to walk every evening before their windows and balconies, without being honoured with a ſingle a ſingle bouquet, though nymphs and flowers were in equal and great abundance.

Among other public buildings, I had almoſt forgot to mention an obſervatory, which ſtands near the middle of the town, and is tolerably well furniſhed with aſtronomical inſtruments. During our ſtay here, ſome Spaniſh and Portugueze mathematicians were endeavouring to determine the boundaries of the territories belonging to their reſpective crowns. Unhappily, however, for the cauſe of ſcience, theſe gentlemen have not hitherto been able to coincide in their accounts, ſo that very little information on this head to be depended upon, could be gained. How far political motives may have cauſed this diſagreement, I do not preſume to decide; though it deſerves notice, that the Portugueze accuſe the Abbé de la Caille, who obſerved here, by order of the King of France, of having laid down the longitude of this place 45 miles too much to the eaſtward.

Until

Until the year 1770, all the flour in the ſettlement was brought from Europe; but ſince that time the inhabitants have made ſo rapid a progreſs in raiſing grain, as to be able to ſupply themſelves with it abundantly. The principal corn country lies around Rio Grande, in the latitude of 32° ſouth, where wheat flouriſhes ſo luxuriantly, as to yield from ſeventy to eighty buſhels for one. Coffee alſo, which they formerly received from Portugal, now grows in ſuch plenty, as to enable them to export conſiderable quantities of it. But the ſtaple commodity of the country is ſugar. That they have not, however, learnt the art of making palatable rum, the Engliſh troops in New South Wales can bear teſtimony; a large quantity, very ill flavoured, having been bought and ſhipped here, for the uſe of the garriſon of Port Jackſon.

It was in 1771 that St. Salvador, which had for more than a century been the capital of Brazil, ceaſed to be ſo; and that the ſeat of Government was removed to St. Sebaſtian. The change took place on account of the colonial war, at that time carried on by the Courts of Liſbon and Madrid. And, indeed, were the object of ſecurity alone to determine the ſeat of Government, I know but few places better ſituated in that reſpect than the one I am deſcribing; the natural ſtrength of the country, joined to the difficulties which would attend an attack on the fortifications, being ſuch as to render it very formidable.

It may be preſumed that the Portugueze Government is well apprized of this circumſtance, and of the little riſque they run in being deprived of ſo important a poſſeſſion, elſe it will not be eaſy to penetrate the reaſons which induce them to treat the troops who compoſe the garriſon, with ſuch cruel negligence. Their regiments were ordered out with a promiſe of being relieved, and ſent back to Europe at the end of three years, in conformity to which they ſettled all their domeſtic arrangements. But the faith of Government has been broken, and at the expiration of twenty years, all that is left to the remnant of theſe unfortunate men, is to ſuffer in ſubmiſſive ſilence. I was one evening walking with a Portugueze officer, when this ſubject was ſtarted, and on my telling him, that ſuch a breach of public honour to Engliſh troops, would become a ſubject of parliamentary inquiry, he ſeized my hand with great eagerneſs, "Ah, Sir!" exclaimed he, "yours is a free "country—we"——His emotions ſpoke what his tongue refuſed.

As I am mentioning the army, I cannot help obſerving, that I ſaw nothing here to confirm the remark of Mr. Cook, that the inhabitants of the place, whenever they meet an officer of the garriſon, bow to him with the greateſt obſequiouſneſs, and by omitting ſuch a ceremony, would ſubject themſelves to be knocked down, though the other ſeldom deigns to return the compliment. The interchange of civilities is general between them, and ſeems by no means extorted. The people who could ſubmit to ſuch inſolent ſuperiority, would, indeed, deſerve to be treated as ſlaves.

The Police of the city is very good, Soldiers patrole the ſtreets frequently, and riots are ſeldom heard of. The dreadful cuſtom of ſtabbing, from motives of private reſentment, is nearly at an end, ſince the church has ceaſed to afford an aſylum to murderers. In other reſpects, the progreſs of improvement appears ſlow, and fettered by obſtacles almoſt unſurmountable, whoſe baneful influence will continue, until a more enlightened ſyſtem of policy ſhall be adopted. From morning to night the ears of a ſtranger are greeted by the tinkling of the convent bells, and his eyes ſaluted by proceſſions of devotees, whoſe adoration and levity ſeem to keep equal pace, and ſucceed each other in turns. " Do you want to make your ſon ſick of ſoldiering? ſhew him the Trainbands of London on a field-day." Let him who would wiſh to give his ſon a diſtaſte to Popery, point out to him the

the ſloth, the ignorance, and the bigotry of this place.

Being nearly ready to depart by the 1ſt of September, as many officers as poſſible went on that day to the palace to take leave of his Excellency, the Viceroy of the Brazils, to whom we had been previouſly introduced; who on this, and every other occaſion, was pleaſed to honour us with the moſt diſtinguiſhed marks of regard and attention. Some part, indeed, of the numerous indulgencies we experienced during our ſtay here, muſt doubtleſs be attributed to the high reſpect in which the Portugueze held Governor Phillip, who was for many years a captain in their navy, and commanded a ſhip of war on this ſtation: in conſequence of which, many privileges were extended to us, very unuſual to be granted to ſtrangers. We were allowed the liberty of making ſhort excurſions into the country, and on theſe occaſions, as well as when walking in the city, the mortifying cuſtom of having an officer

officer of the garrison attending us was dispensed with on our leaving our names and ranks, at the time of landing, with the adjutant of orders at the palace. It happened, however, sometimes, that the presence of a military man was necessary, to prevent imposition in the shopkeepers, who frequently made a practice of asking more for their goods than the worth of them. In which case an officer, when applied to, always told us the usual price of the commodity with the greatest readiness, and adjusted the terms of the purchase.

On the morning of the fourth [September] we left Rio de Janeiro, amply furnished with the good things which its happy soil and clime so abundantly produce. The future voyager may with security depend on this place for laying in many parts of his stock. Among these may be enumerated sugar, coffee, rum, port wine, rice, tapioca, and tobacco, besides very beautiful wood for the purposes of houshold furniture. Poultry is not remarkably cheap, but may be procured

in

in any quantity; as may hops at a low rate. The markets are well ſupplied with butcher's meat, and vegetables of every ſort are to be procured at a price next to nothing; the yams are particularly excellent. Oranges abound ſo much, as to be ſold for ſixpence a hundred; and limes are to be had on terms equally moderate. Bananas, cocoa nuts, and guavas, are common; but the few pine-apples brought to market are not remarkable either for flavour, or cheapneſs. Beſides the inducements to lay out money already mentioned, the naturaliſt may add to his collection by an almoſt endleſs variety of beautiful birds, and curious inſects, which are to be bought at a reaſonable price, well preſerved, and neatly aſſorted.

I ſhall cloſe my account of this place by informing ſtrangers, who may come here, that the Portugueze reckon their money in rees, an imaginary coin, twenty of which make a ſmall copper piece called a vintin, and ſixteen of theſe laſt a petack. Every piece is marked with the number of

rees

rees it is worth, ſo that a miſtake can hardly happen. Engliſh ſilver coin has loſt its reputation here, and dollars will be found preferable to any other money.

CHAP. VI.

The Paſſage from the Brazils *to the* Cape of Good Hope; *with an Account of the Tranſactions of the Fleet there.*

September 1787.

OUR paſſage from Rio de Janeiro to the Cape of Good Hope was equally proſperous with that which had preceded it. We ſteered away to the ſouth-eaſt, and loſt ſight of the American coaſt the day after our departure. From this time until the 13th of October, when we made the Cape, nothing remarkable occurred, except the loſs of a convict in the ſhip I was on board, who unfortunately fell into the ſea, and periſhed in ſpite of our efforts to ſave him, by cutting adrift a life buoy and hoiſting out a boat. During the paſſage, a ſlight dyſentery prevailed in ſome of the ſhips, but was in no inſtance mortal. We were at firſt inclined to impute it to the water we took on board at the Brazils, but as the effect was very partial, ſome other cauſe was more probably the occaſion of it.

At ſeven o'clock in the evening of the 13th of October, we caſt anchor in Table Bay, and found many ſhips of different nations in the harbour.

Little can be added to the many accounts already publiſhed of the Cape of Good Hope, though, if an opinion on the ſubject might be riſqued, the deſcriptions they contain are too flattering. When contraſted with Rio de Janeiro it certainly ſuffers in the compariſon. Indeed, we arrived at a time equally unfavourable for judging of the produce of the ſoil and the temper of its cultivators, who had ſuffered conſiderably, from a dearth that had happened the preceding ſeaſon, and created a general ſcarcity. Nor was the chagrin of theſe deprivations leſſened by the news daily arriving of the convulſions that ſhook the republic, which could not fail to make an impreſſion even on Batavian phlegm.

As

As a conſiderable quantity of flour, and the principal part of the live ſtock, which was to ſtore our intended ſettlement, were meant to be procured here, Governor Phillip loſt no time in waiting on Mynheer Van Graaffe, the Dutch Governor, to requeſt permiſſion (according to the cuſtom of the place) to purchaſe all that we ſtood in need of. How far the demand extended, I know not, nor Mynheer Van Graaffe's reaſons for complying with it in part only. To this gentleman's political ſentiments I confeſs myſelf a ſtranger, though I ſhould do his politeneſs and liberality at his own table an injuſtice, were I not to take this public opportunity of acknowledging them; nor can I reſiſt the opportunity which preſents itſelf, to inform my readers, in honor of M. Van Graaffe's humanity, that he has made repeated efforts to recover the unfortunate remains of the crew of the Groſvenor Indiaman, which was wrecked about five years ago on the coaſt of Caffraria. This information was given me by Colonel Gordon, commandant of the Dutch troops at the Cape, whoſe knowledge of the interior parts of this country ſurpaſſes that of any other man. And I am ſorry to ſay, that the Colonel added, theſe unhappy people were irrecoverably loſt to the world and their friends, by being detained among the Caffres, the moſt ſavage ſet of brutes on earth.

His Excellency reſides at the government houſe, in the Eaſt India Company's garden. This laſt is of conſiderable extent, and is planted chiefly with vegetables for the Dutch Indiamen which may happen to touch at the port. Some of the walks are extremely pleaſant, from the ſhade they afford, and the whole garden is very neatly kept. The regular lines interſecting each other at right angles, in which it is laid out, will, nevertheleſs, afford but little gratification to an Engliſhman, who has been uſed to contemplate the natural ſtyle which diſtinguiſhes the pleaſure grounds of his own country. At the head of the center walks ſtands a menagerie, on which, as well as the garden, many pompous eulogiums have been paſſed, though in my own judgement, conſidering the local advantages poſſeſſed by the com-

company, it is poorly furniſhed both with animals and birds: a tyger, a zebra, ſome fine oſtriches, a caſſowary, and the lovely crown-fowl, are among the moſt remarkable.

The table land, which ſtands at the back of the town, is a black dreary looking mountain, apparently flat at top, and of more than eleven hundred yards in height. The guſts of wind which blow from it are violent to an exceſs, and have a very unpleaſant effect, by raiſing the duſt in ſuch clouds, as to render ſtirring out of doors next to impoſſible. Nor can any precaution prevent the inhabitants from being annoyed by it, as much within doors as without.

At length the wiſhed-for day, on which the next effort for reaching the place of our deſtination was to be made, appeared. The morning was calm, but the land wind getting up about noon, on the 12th of November we weighed anchor, and ſoon left far behind every ſcene of civilization and hu-

manized

manized manners, to explore a remote and barbarous land; and plant in it thoſe happy arts, which alone conſtitute the pre-eminence and dignity of other countries.

The live animals we took on board on the public account from the Cape, for ſtocking our projected colony, were, two bulls, three cows, three horſes, forty-four ſheep, and thirty-two hogs, beſides goats, and a very large quantity of poultry of every kind. A conſiderable addition to this was made by the private ſtocks of the officers, who were, however, under a neceſſity of circumſcribing their original intentions on this head very much, from the exceſſive dearneſs of many of the articles. It will readily be believed, that few of the military found it convenient to purchaſe ſheep, when hay to feed them coſts ſixteen ſhillings a hundred weight.

The boarding houſes on ſhore, to which ſtrangers have recourſe, are more reaſonable than might be expected. For a dollar and a half per day we were well lodged, and partook of a table tolerably ſupplied in the French ſtyle. Should a traveller's ſtock of tea run ſhort, it is a thouſand chances to one, that he will be able to repleniſh it here, at a cheaper rate than in England. He may procure plenty of arrack and white wine, alſo raiſins, and dried fruits of other ſorts. If he diſlikes to live at a boarding houſe, he will find the markets well ſtored, and the price of butcher's meat and vegetables far from exceſſive.

Juſt before the ſignal for weighing was made, a ſhip, under American colours, entered the road, bound from Boſton, from whence ſhe had ſailed one hundred and forty days, on a trading voyage to the Eaſt Indies. In her route, ſhe had been lucky enough to pick up ſeveral of the inferior officers and crew of the Harcourt Eaſt-Indiaman, which ſhip had been wrecked on one of the Cape de Verd iſlands. The maſter, who appeared to be a man of ſome information, on being told the deſtination of our fleet, gave it as his opinion, that if a reception could be ſecu-

red,

red, emigrations would take place to New South Wales, not only from the old continent, but the new one, where the ſpirit of adventure and thirſt for novelty were exceſſive.

CHAP.

CHAP. VII.

The Paſſage from the Cape of Good Hope *to* Botany Bay.

November, 1787.

WE had hardly cleared the land when a ſouth-eaſt wind ſet in, and, except at ſhort intervals, continued to blow until the 19th of the month; when we were in the latitude of 37° 40′ ſouth, and, by the time-keeper, in longitude 11° 30′ eaſt, ſo that our diſtance from Botany Bay had increaſed nearly an hundred leagues, ſince leaving the Cape. As no appearance of a change in our favour ſeemed likely to take place, Governor Phillip at this time ſignified his intention of ſhifting his pennant from the Sirius to the Supply, and proceeding on his voyage without waiting for the reſt of the fleet, which was formed in two diviſions. The firſt conſiſting of three tranſports, known to be the beſt ſailors, was put under the command of a Lieutenant of the navy; and the remaining three, with the victuallers, left in charge of Captain Hunter, of his Majeſty's ſhip Sirius. In the laſt diviſion was the veſſel, in which the author of this narrative ſerved. Various cauſes prevented the ſeparation from taking place until the 25th, when ſeveral ſawyers, carpenters, blackſmiths, and other mechanics, were ſhifted from different ſhips into the Supply, in order to facilitate his Excellency's intention of forwarding the neceſſary buildings to be erected at Botany Bay, by the time the reſt of the fleet might be expected to arrive. Lieutenant Governor Roſs, and the Staff of the marine battalion, alſo removed from the Sirius into the Scarborough tranſport, one of the ſhips of the firſt diviſion, in order to afford every aſſiſtance which the public ſervice might receive, by their being early on the ſpot on which our future operations were to be conducted.

From this time a ſucceſſion of fair winds and pleaſant weather correſponded to our eager deſires, and on the 7th of January, 1788, the long wiſhed for ſhore of Van Diemen

Diemen gratified our ſight. We made the land at two o'clock in the afternoon, the very hour we expected to ſee it from the lunar obſervations of Captain Hunter, whoſe accuracy, as an aſtronomer, and conduct as an officer, had inſpired us with equal gratitude and admiration.

After ſo long a confinement, on a ſervice ſo peculiarly diſguſting and troubleſome, it cannot be matter of ſurpriſe that we were overjoyed at the near proſpect of a change of ſcene. By ſunſet we had paſſed between the rocks, which Captain Furneaux named the Mewſton and Swilly. The former bears a very cloſe reſemblance to the little iſland near Plymouth, whence it took its name; its latitude is 43° 48′ ſouth, longitude 146° 25′ eaſt of Greenwich.

In running along ſhore, we caſt many an anxious eye towards the land, on which ſo much of our future deſtiny depended. Our diſtance, joined to the hazineſs of the atmoſphere, prevented us, however, from being able to diſcover much. With our beſt

 glaſſes

glaſſes we could ſee nothing but hills of a moderate height, cloathed with trees, to which ſome little patches of white ſand-ſtone gave the appearance of being covered with ſnow. Many fires were obſerved on the hills in the evening.

As no perſon in the ſhip I was on board had been on this coaſt before, we conſulted a little chart, publiſhed by Steele of the Minories, London, and found it, in general, very correct; it would be more ſo, were not the Mewſtone laid down at too great a diſtance from the land, and one object made of the Eddyſtone and Swilly, when, in fact, they are diſtinct. Between the two laſt is an entire bed of impaſſable rocks, many of them above water The latitude of the Eddyſtone is 43° 53½′, longitude 147° 9′; that of Swilly 43° 54′ ſouth, longitude 147° 3′ eaſt of Greenwich.

In the night the weſterly wind, which had ſo long befriended us, died away, and was ſucceeded by one from the north-eaſt. When day appeared we had loſt ſight of the

 land,

land, and did not regain it until the 19th, at only the diſtance of 17 leagues from our deſired port. The wind was now fair, the ſky ſerene, though a little hazy, and the temperature of the air delightfully pleaſant: joy ſparkled in every countenance, and congratulations iſſued from every mouth. Ithaca itſelf was ſcarcely more longed for by Ulyſſes, than Botany Bay by the adventurers who had traverſed ſo many thouſand miles to take poſſeſſion of it.

"Heavily in clouds came on the day" which uſhered in our arrival. To us it was "a great, an important day," though I hope the foundation, not the fall, of an empire will be dated from it.

On the morning of the 20th, by ten o'clock, the whole of the fleet had caſt anchor in Botany Bay, where, to our mutual ſatisfaction, we found the Governor, and the firſt diviſion of tranſports. On inquiry, we heard, that the Supply had arrived on the 18th, and the tranſports only the preceding day.

Thus,

Thus, after a paſſage of exactly thirty-ſix weeks from Portſmouth, we happily effected our arduous undertaking, with ſuch a train of unexampled bleſſings, as hardly ever attended a fleet in a like predicament. Of two hundred and twelve marines we loſt only one; and of ſeven hundred and ſeventy-five convicts, put on board in England, but twenty-four periſhed in our route. To what cauſe are we to attribute this unhoped for ſucceſs? I wiſh I could anſwer to the liberal manner in which Government ſupplied the expedition. But when the reader is told, that ſome of the neceſſary articles allowed to ſhips on a common paſſage to the Weſt Indies, were with-held from us; that portable ſoup, wheat, and pickled vegetables were not allowed; and that an inadequate quantity of eſſence of malt was the only antiſcorbutic ſupplied, his ſurpriſe will redouble at the reſult of the voyage. For it muſt be remembered, that the people thus ſent out were not a ſhip's company ſtarting with every advantage of health and good living, which a ſtate of freedom produces; but the major part a miſerable ſet of convicts,

emaciated

emaciated from confinement, and in want of cloaths, and almoſt every convenience to render ſo long a paſſage tolerable. I beg leave, however, to ſay, that the proviſions ſerved on board were good, and of a much ſuperior quality to thoſe uſually ſupplied by contract: they were furniſhed by Meſſrs. Richards and Thorn, of Tower-ſtreet, London.

C H. A P. IX.

From the Fleet's Arrival at Botany Bay, *to the Evacuation of it; and taking Poſſeſſion of* Port Jackſon. *Interviews with the Natives; and an Account of the Country about* Botany Bay.

January, 1788.

WE had ſcarcely bid each other welcome on our arrival, when an expedition up the Bay was undertaken by the Governor and Lieutenant-Governor, in order to explore the nature of the country, and fix on a ſpot to begin our operations upon. None, however, which could be deemed very eligible, being diſcovered, his Excellency proceeded in a boat to examine the opening, to which Mr. Cook had given the name of Port Jackſon, on an idea that a ſhelter for ſhipping within it might be found. The boat returned on the evening of the 23d, with ſuch an account of the harbour and advantages attending the place, that it was deter-

determined the evacuation of Botany Bay ſhould commence the next morning.

In conſequence of this deciſion, the few ſeamen and marines who had been landed from the ſquadron, were inſtantly reimbarked, and every preparation made to bid adieu to a port which had ſo long been the ſubject of our converſation; which but three days before we had entered with ſo many ſentiments of ſatisfaction; and in which, as we had believed, ſo many of our future hours were to be paſſed. The thoughts of removal baniſhed ſleep, ſo that I roſe at the firſt dawn of the morning. But judge of my ſurprize on hearing from a ſerjeant, who ran down almoſt breathleſs to the cabin where I was dreſſing, that a ſhip was ſeen off the harbour's mouth. At firſt I only laughed, but knowing the man who ſpcke to me to be of great veracity, and hearing him repeat his information, I flew upon deck, on which I had barely ſet my foot, when the cry of "another ſail" ſtruck on my aſtoniſhed ear. Confounded by a thouſand ideas which aroſe in my mind in an inſtant, I ſprang upon the barricado, and plainly descried two ships of considerable size, standing in for the mouth of the Bay. By this time the alarm had become general, and every one appeared lost in conjecture. Now they were Dutchmen sent to dispossess us, and the moment after storeships from England, with supplies for the settlement. The improbabilities which attended both these conclusions, were sunk in the agitation of the moment. It was by Governor Phillip, that this mystery was at length unravelled, and the cause of the alarm pronounced to be two French ships, it was now recollected were on a voyage of discovery in the southern hemisphere. Thus were our doubts cleared up, and our apprehensions banished; it was, however, judged expedient to postpone our removal to Port Jackson, until a complete confirmation of our conjectures could be procured.

Had the sea breeze set in, the strange ships would have been at anchor in the Bay by eight o'clock in the morning, but the wind blowing out, they were driven by a strong a ſtrong lee current to the ſouthward of the port. On the following day they re-appeared in their former ſituation, and a boat was ſent to them, with a lieutenant of the navy in her, to offer aſſiſtance, and point out the neceſſary marks for entering the harbour. In the courſe of the day the officer returned, and brought intelligence that the ſhips were the Bouſſole and Aſtrolabe, ſent out by order of the King of France, and under the command of Monſieur De Perrouſe. The aſtoniſhment of the French at ſeeing us, had not equalled that we had experienced, for it appeared, that in the courſe of their voyage they had touched at Kamſchatka, and by that means learnt that our expedition was in contemplation. They dropped anchor the next morning, juſt as we had got under weigh to work out of the Bay, ſo that for the preſent nothing more than ſalutations could paſs between us.

Before I quit Botany Bay, I ſhall relate the obſervations we were enabled to make during our ſhort ſtay there; as well as thoſe which our ſubſequent viſits to it from Port Jackſon enabled us to complete.

The Bay is very open, and greatly expoſed to the fury of the S. E. winds, which when they blow, cauſe a heavy and dangerous ſwell. It is of prodigious extent, the principal arm, which takes a S. W. direction, being not leſs, including its windings, than twenty-four miles from the capes which form the entrance, according to the report of the French officers, who took uncommon pains to ſurvey it. At the diſtance of a league from the harbour's mouth is a bar, on which at low water, not more than fifteen feet are to be found. Within this bar, for many miles up the S. W. arm, is a haven, equal in every reſpect to any hitherto known, and in which any number of ſhips might anchor, ſecured from all winds. The country around far exceeds in richneſs of ſoil that about Cape Banks and Point Solander, though unfortunately they reſemble each other in one reſpect, a ſcarcity of freſh water.

We

We found the natives tolerably numerous as we advanced up the river, and even at the harbour's mouth we had reaſon to conclude the country more populous than Mr. Cook thought it. For on the Supply's arrival in the Bay on the 18th of the month, they were aſſembled on the beach of the ſouth ſhore, to the number of not leſs than forty perſons, ſhouting and making many uncouth ſigns and geſtures. This appearance whetted curioſity to its utmoſt, but as prudence forbade a few people to venture wantonly among ſo great a number, and a party of only ſix men was obſerved on the north ſhore, the Governor immediately proceeded to land on that ſide, in order to take poſſeſſion of his new territory, and bring about an intercourſe between its old and new maſters. The boat, in which his Excellency was, rowed up the harbour, cloſe to the land, for ſome diſtance; the Indians keeping pace with her on the beach. At laſt an officer in the boat made ſigns of a want of water, which it was judged would indicate his wiſh of landing. The natives directly comprehended what he wanted, and

pointed

pointed to a ſpot where water could be procured: on which the boat was immediately puſhed in, and a landing took place. As on the event of this meeting might depend ſo much of our future tranquillity, every delicacy on our ſide was requiſite. The Indians, though timorous, ſhewed no ſigns of reſentment at the Governor's going on ſhore; an interview commenced, in which the conduct of both parties pleaſed each other ſo much, that the ſtrangers returned to their ſhips with a much better opinion of the natives, than they had landed with; and the latter ſeemed highly entertained with their new acquaintance, from whom they condeſcended to accept of a looking-glaſs, ſome beads, and other toys.

Owing to the lateneſs of our arrival, it was not my good fortune to go on ſhore until three days after this had happened, when I went with a party to the ſouth ſide of the harbour, and had ſcarcely landed five minutes, when we were met by a dozen Indians, naked as at the moment of their birth, walking along the beach. Eager to

come

come to a conference, and yet afraid of giving offence, we advanced with caution towards them, nor would they, at firſt, approach nearer to us than the diſtance of ſome paces. Both parties were armed; yet an attack ſeemed as unlikely on their part, as we knew it to be on our own. I had at this time a little boy, of not more than ſeven years of age, in my hand. The child ſeemed to attract their attention very much, for they frequently pointed to him and ſpoke to each other; and as he was not frightened, I advanced with him towards them, at the ſame time baring his boſom and ſhewing the whiteneſs of the ſkin. On the cloaths being removed they gave a loud exclamation, and one of the party, an old man, with a long beard, hideouſly ugly, came cloſe to us. I bade my little charge not to be afraid, and introduced him to the acquaintance of this uncouth perſonage. The Indian, with great gentleneſs, laid his hand on the child's hat, and afterwards felt his cloaths, muttering to himſelf all the while. I found it neceſſary, however, by this time to ſend away the child, as ſuch a cloſe

close connection rather alarmed him, and in this, as the conclusion verified, I gave no offence to the old gentleman. Indeed it was but putting ourselves on a par with them, as I had observed from the first, that some youths of their own, though considerably older than the one with us, were kept back by the grown people. Several more now came up, to whom we made various presents, but our toys seemed not to be regarded as very valuable; nor would they for a long time make any returns to them, though before we parted, a large club, with a head almost sufficient to fell an ox, was obtained in exchange for a looking-glass. These people seemed at a loss to know (probably from our want of beards) of what sex we were, which having understood, they burst into the most immoderate fits of laughter, talking to each other at the same time with such rapidity and vociferation as I had never before heard. After nearly an hour's conversation by signs and gestures, they repeated several times the word *whurra*, which signifies, begone, and walked away from us to the head of the Bay.

The natives being departed, we ſet out to obſerve the country, which, on inſpection, rather diſappointed our hopes, being invariably ſandy and unpromiſing for the purpoſes of cultivation, though the trees and graſs flouriſh in great luxuriancy. Cloſe to us was the ſpring at which Mr. Cook watered, but we did not think the water very excellent, nor did it run freely. In the evening we returned on board, not greatly pleaſed with the latter part of our diſcoveries, as it indicated an increaſe of thoſe difficulties, which before ſeemed ſufficiently numerous.

Between this and our departure we had ſeveral more interviews with the natives, which ended in ſo friendly a manner, that we began to entertain ſtrong hopes of bringing about a connection with them. Our firſt object was to win their affections, and our next to convince them of the ſuperiority we poſſeſſed: for without the latter, the former we knew would be of little importance. An officer one day prevailed on one of them to place a target, made of bark,

 againſt

againſt a tree, which he fired at with a piſtol, at the diſtance of ſome paces. The Indians, though terrified at the report, did not run away, but their aſtoniſhment exceeded their alarm, on looking at the ſhield which the ball had perforated. As this produced a little ſhyneſs, the officer, to diſſipate their fears and remove their jealouſy, whiſtled the air of *Malbrooke*, which they appeared highly charmed with, and imitated him with equal pleaſure and readineſs. I cannot help remarking here, what I was afterwards told by Monſieur De Perrouſe, that the natives of California, and throughout all the iſlands of the Pacific Ocean, and in ſhort wherever he had been, ſeemed equally touched and delighted with this little plaintive air.

CHAP.

CHAP. IX.

The taking Poſſeſſion of Port Jackſon. *With the Diſembarkation of the Marines and Convicts.*

January, 1788.

OUR paſſage to Port Jackſon took up but few hours, and thoſe were ſpent far from unpleaſantly. The evening was bright, and the proſpect before us ſuch as might juſtify ſanguine expectation. Having paſſed between the capes which form its entrance, we found ourſelves in a port ſuperior, in extent and excellency, to all we had ſeen before. We continued to run up the harbour about four miles, in a weſterly direction, enjoying the luxuriant proſpect of its ſhores, covered with trees to the water's edge, among which many of the Indians were frequently ſeen, till we arrived at a ſmall ſnug cove on the ſouthern ſide, on whoſe banks the plan of our operations was deſtined to commence.

The landing of a part of the marines and convicts took place the next day, and on the following, the remainder was diſembarked. Buſineſs now ſat on every brow, and the ſcene, to an indifferent ſpectator, at leiſure to contemplate it, would have been highly pictureſque and amuſing. In one place, a party cutting down the woods; a ſecond, ſetting up a blackſmith's forge; a third, dragging along a load of ſtones or proviſions; here an officer pitching his marquee, with a detachment of troops parading on one ſide of him, and a cook's fire blazing up on the other. Through the unwearied diligence of thoſe at the head of the different departments, regularity was, however, ſoon introduced, and, as far as the unſettled ſtate of matters would allow, confuſion gave place to ſyſtem.

Into the head of the cove, on which our eſtabliſhment is fixed, runs a ſmall ſtream of freſh water, which ſerves to divide the adjacent

adjacent country to a little diſtance, in the direction of north and ſouth. On the eaſtern ſide of this rivulet the Governor fixed his place of reſidence, with a large body of convicts encamped near him; and on the the weſtern ſide was diſpoſed the remaining part of theſe peole, near the marine encampment. From this laſt two guards, conſiſting of two ſubalterns, as many ſerjeants, four corporals, two drummers, and forty-two private men, under the orders of a Captain of the day, to whom all reports were made, daily mounted for the public ſecurity, with ſuch directions to uſe force, in caſe of neceſſity, as left no room for thoſe who were the object of the order, but to remain peaceable, or periſh by the bayonet.

As the ſtraggling of the convicts was not only a deſertion from the public labour, but might be attended with ill conſequences to the ſettlement, in caſe of their meeting the natives, every care was taken to prevent it. The Provoſt Martial with his men was ordered to patrole the country around, and the

the convicts informed, that the severest punishment would be inflicted on transgressors. In spite, however, of all our precautions, they soon found the road to Botany Bay, in visits to the French, who would gladly have dispensed with their company.

But as severity alone was known to be inadequate at once to chastize and reform, no opportunity was omitted to assure the convicts, that by their good behaviour and submissive deportment, every claim to present distinction and future favour was to be earned. That this caution was not attended with all the good effects which were hoped from it, I have only to lament; that it operated in some cases is indisputable; nor will a candid and humane mind fail to consider and allow for the situation these unfortunate beings so peculiarly stood in. While they were on board ship, the two sexes had been kept most rigorously apart; but, when landed, their separation became impracticable, and would have been, perhaps, wrong. Licentiousneſs was the unavoidable conſequence, and their old habits of depravity were beginning to recur. What was to be attempted? To prevent their intercourſe was impoſſible; and to palliate its evils only remained. Marriage was recommended, and ſuch advantages held out to thoſe who aimed at reformation, as have greatly contributed to the tranquillity of the ſettlement.

On the Sunday after our landing divine ſervice was performed under a great tree, by the Rev. Mr. Johnſon, Chaplain of the Settlement, in the preſence of the troops and convicts, whoſe behaviour on the occaſion was equally regular and attentive. In the courſe of our paſſage this had been repeated every Sunday, while the ſhips were in port; and in addition to it, Mr. Johnſon had furniſhed them with books, at once tending to promote inſtruction and piety.

The Indians for a little while after our arrival paid us frequent viſits, but in a few days they were obſerved to be more ſhy of our company. From what cauſe their diſ-

taſte

taſte aroſe we never could trace, as we had made it our ſtudy, on theſe occaſions, to treat them with kindneſs, and load them with preſents. No quarrel had happened, and we had flattered ourſelves, from Governor Phillip's firſt reception among them, that ſuch a connection might be eſtabliſhed as would tend to the intereſt of both parties. It ſeems, that on that occaſion, they not only received our people with great cordiality, but ſo far acknowledged their authority as to ſubmit, that a boundary, during their firſt interview, might be drawn on the ſand, which they attempted not to infringe, and appeared to be ſatisfied with.

CHAP. X.

February, 1788.

The Reading of the Commissions, and taking Possession of the Settlement, in form. With an Account of the Courts of Law, and Mode of administering Public Justice in this Country.

OWING to the multiplicity of pressing business necessary to be performed immediately after landing, it was found impossible to read the public commissions and take possession of the colony in form, until the 7th of February. On that day all the officers of guard took post in the marine battalion, which was drawn up, and marched off the parade with music playing, and colours flying, to an adjoining ground, which had been cleared for the occasion, whereon the convicts were assembled to hear His Majesty's commission read, appointing his Excellency Arthur Phillip, Esq. Governor and Captain General in and over the territory of New

South Wales, and its dependencies; together with the Act of Parliament for eſtabliſhing trials by law within the ſame; and the patents under the Great Seal of Great Britain, for holding the civil and criminal courts of judicature, by which all caſes of life and death, as well as matters of property, were to be decided. When the Judge Advocate had finiſhed reading, his Excellency addreſſed himſelf to the convicts in a pointed and judicious ſpeech, informing them of his future intentions, which were, invariably to cheriſh and render happy thoſe who ſhewed a diſpoſition to amendment; and to let the rigour of the law take its courſe againſt ſuch as might dare to tranſgreſs the bounds preſcribed. At the cloſe three vollies were fired in honour of the occaſion, and the battalion marched back to their parade, where they were reviewed by the Governor, who was received with all the honours due to his rank. His Excellency was afterwards pleaſed to thank them, in public orders, for their behaviour from the time of their embarkation; and to aſk the officers to partake of a cold collation, at which

which it is ſcarce neceſſary to obſerve, that many loyal and public toaſts were drank in commemoration of the day.

In the Governor's commiſſion, the extent of this authority is defined to reach from the latitude of 43° 49 ſouth, to the latitude of 10° 37′ ſouth, being the northern and ſouthern extremities of the continent of New Holland. It commences again at 135th degree of longitude eaſt of Greenwich, and proceeding in an eaſterly direction, includes all iſlands within the limits of the above ſpecified latitudes in the Pacific ocean. By this partition it may be fairly preſumed, that every ſource of future litigation between the Dutch and us will be for ever cut off, as the diſcoveries of Engliſh navigators alone are comprized in this territory.

Nor have Government been more backward in arming Mr. Phillip with plenitude of power, than extent of dominion. No mention is made of a Council to be appointed, ſo that he is left to act entirely from his own judgement. And as no ſtated time of aſſembling the Courts of Juſtice is pointed out, ſimilar to the aſſizes and gaol deliveries of England, the duration of imprisonment is altogether in his hands. The power of ſummoning General Courts Martial to meet he is alſo inveſted with, but the inſertion in the marine mutiny act, of a ſmaller number of officers than thirteen being able to compoſe ſuch a tribunal, has been neglected: ſo that a military court, ſhould detachments be made from head-quarters, or ſickneſs prevail, may not always be found practicable to be obtained, unleſs the number of officers, at preſent in the Settlement, ſhall be increaſed.

Should the Governor ſee cauſe, he is enabled to grant pardons to offenders convicted, " in all caſes whatever, treaſon and wilful " murder excepted," and even in theſe, has authority to ſtay the execution of the law, until the King's pleaſure ſhall be ſignified. In caſe of the Governor's death, the Lieutenant Governor takes his place; and on his demiſe, the ſenior officer on the ſpot is authoriſed to aſſume the reins of power.

Not-

Notwithſtanding the promiſes made on one ſide, and the forbearance ſhewn on the other, joined to the impending rod of juſtice, it was with infinite regret that every one ſaw, in four days afterwards, the neceſſity of aſſembling a Criminal Court, which was accordingly convened by warrant from the Governor, and conſiſted of the Judge Advocate, who preſided, three naval, and three marine officers.

As the conſtitution of this court is altogether new in the Britiſh annals, I hope my reader will not think me prolix in the deſcription I am about to give of it. The number of members, including the Judge Advocate, is limited, by Act of Parliament, to ſeven, who are expreſſly ordered to be officers, either of His Majeſty's ſea or land forces. The court being met, completely arrayed and armed as at a military tribunal, the Judge Advocate proceeds to adminiſter the uſual oath taken by jurymen in England to each member; one of whom afterwards ſwears him in a like manner. This ceremony being adjuſted, the crime laid to the pri-

priſoner's charge is read to him, and the queſtion of Guilty, or Not guilty, put. No law officer on the ſide of the crown being appointed, (for I preſume the head of the court ought hardly to conſider himſelf in that light, notwithſtanding the title he bears) to proſecute the criminal is left entirely to the party, at whoſe ſuit he is tried. All the witneſſes are examined on oath, and the deciſion is directed to be given according to the laws of England, " or as nearly as may be, allowing for the circum-" ſtances and ſituation of the ſettlement," by " a majority of votes, beginning with the youngeſt member, and ending with the preſident of the court. In caſes, however, of a capital nature, no verdict can be given, unleſs five, at leaſt, of the ſeven members preſent concur therein. The evidence on both ſides being finiſhed, and the priſoner's defence heard, the court is cleared, and on the judgement being ſettled, is thrown open again, and ſentence pronounced. During the time the court ſits, the place in which it is aſſembled is directed to be ſurrounded by a guard under arms, and admiſſion to every

every one who may chooſe to enter it, granted. Of late, however, our coloniſts are ſuppoſed to be in ſuch a train of ſubordination, as to make the preſence of ſo large a military force unneceſſary; and two centinels, in addition to the Provoſt Martial, are conſidered as ſufficient.

It would be as needleſs, as impertinent, to anticipate the reflections which will ariſe in reading the above account, wherein a regard to accuracy only has been conſulted. By comparing it with the mode of adminiſtering juſtice in the Engliſh courts of law, it will be found to differ in many points very eſſentially. And if we turn our eyes to the uſage of military tribunals, it no leſs departs from the cuſtoms obſerved in them. Let not the novelty of it, however, prejudice any one ſo far as to diſpute its efficacy, and the neceſſity of the caſe which gave it birth.

The court, whoſe meeting is already ſpoken of, proceeded to the trial of three convicts, one of whom was convicted of having ſtruck a marine with a cooper's adze, and otherwiſe behaving in a very riotous and ſcandalous manner, for which he was ſentenced to receive one hundred and fifty laſhes, being a ſmaller puniſhment than a ſoldier in a like caſe would have ſuffered from the judgement of a court martial. A ſecond for having committed a petty theft, was ſent to a ſmall barren iſland, and kept there on bread and water only, for a week. And the third was ſentenced to receive fifty laſhes, but was recommended by the court to the Governor, and forgiven.

Hitherto, however, [February] nothing of a very atrocious nature had appeared. But the day was at hand, on which the violation of public ſecurity could no longer be reſtrained, by the infliction of temporary puniſhment. A ſet of deſperate and hardened villains, leagued themſelves for the purpoſes of depredation, and, as it generally happens, had art enough to perſuade ſome others leſs deeply verſed in iniquity, to be the inſtruments for carrying it on. Fortunately the porgreſs of theſe miſcreants was not of long duration. They

were

were detected in ſtealing a large quantity of proviſions at the time of iſſuing them. And on being apprehended, one of the tools of the ſuperiors impeached the reſt, and diſcloſed the ſcheme. The trial came on the 28th of the month, and of four who were arraigned for the offence, three were condemned to die, and the fourth to receive a very ſevere corporal puniſhment. In hopes that his lenity would not be abuſed, his Excellency was, however, pleaſed to order one only for execution, which took place a little before ſun-ſet the ſame day. The name of the unhappy wretch was, Thomas Barret, an old and deſperate offender, who died with that hardy ſpirit, which too often is found in the worſt and moſt abandoned claſs of men; during the execution the battalion of marines was under arms, and the whole of the convicts obliged to be preſent. The two aſſociates of the ſufferer were ordered to be kept cloſe priſoners, until an eligible place to baniſh them to could be fixed on; as were alſo two more, who on the following day were condemned to die for a ſimilar offence.

Beſides the Criminal court, there is an inferior one, compoſed of the Judge Advocate, and one or more juſtices of the peace, for the trial of ſmall miſdemeanours. This court is likewiſe empowered to decide all law ſuits, and its verdict is final, except where the ſum in diſpute amounts to more than three hundred pounds, in which caſe an appeal to England can be made from its decree. Should neceſſity warrant it, an Admiralty court, of which Lieutenant Governor Roſs is judge, can alſo be ſummoned, for the trial of offences committed on the high ſeas.

From being unwilling to break the thread of my narrative, I omitted to note in its proper place the ſailing of the Supply, Lieut. Ball, on the 15th of the month, for Norfolk Iſland, which the Governor had inſtructions from the miniſtry to take poſſeſſion of. Lieut. King of the Sirius was ſent as ſuperintendant and commandant of this place, and carried with him a ſurgeon, a midſhipman, a ſawyer, a weaver, two marines, and ſixteen convicts, of whom ſix were women. He was alſo ſupplied with a certain number of live animals to ſtock the iſland, beſides garden ſeeds, grain, and other requiſites.

CHAP. XI.

A Deſcription of the Natives of New South Wales, *and our Tranſactions with them.*

I DOUBT not my readers will be as glad as I feel myſelf, to conclude the dull detail of the laſt chapter. If they pleaſe, they may turn from the ſubtle intricacies of the law, to contemplate the ſimple undiſguiſed workings of nature, in her moſt artleſs colouring.

I have already ſaid, we had been but very few days at Port Jackſon, when an alteration in the behaviour of the natives was perceptible; and I wiſh I could add, that a longer reſidence in their neighbourhood had introduced a greater degree of cordiality and intermixture between the old, and new, lords of the ſoil, than at the day on which this publication is dated ſubſiſts.

From

From their eafy reception of us in the beginning, many were induced to call in queftion the accounts which Mr. Cook had given of this people. That celebrated navigator, we were willing to believe, had fomehow by his conduct offended them, which prevented the intercourfe that would otherwife have taken place. The refult, however, of our repeated endeavours to induce them to come among us has been fuch as to confirm me in an opinion, that they either fear or defpife us too much, to be anxious for a clofer connection. And I beg leave at once, to apprize the reader, that all I can here, or in any future part of this work, relate with fidelity of the natives of New South Wales, muft be made up of detached obfervations, taken at different times, and not from a regular feries of knowledge of the cuftoms and manners of a people, with whom opportunities of communication are fo fcarce, as to have been feldom obtained.

In their perfons, they are far from being a ftout race of men, though nimble, fprightly, ly, and vigorous. The deficiency of one of the fore teeth of the upper jaw, mentioned by Dampier, we have ſeen in almoſt the whole of the men; but their organs of ſight, ſo far from being defective, as that author mentions thoſe of the inhabitants of the weſtern ſide of the continent to be, are remarkably quick and piercing. Their colour, Mr. Cook is inclined to think rather a deep chocolate, than an abſolute black, though he confeſſes, they have the appearance of the latter, which he attributes to the greaſy filth their ſkins are loaded with. Of their want of cleanlineſs we have had ſufficient proofs, but I am of opinion, all the waſhing in the world would not render them two degrees leſs black than an African negro. At ſome of our firſt interviews, we had ſeveral droll inſtances of their miſtaking the Africans we brought with us for their own countrymen.

Notwithſtanding the diſregard they have invariably ſhewn for all the finery we could deck them with, they are fond of adorning themſelves with ſcars, which increaſe their natural hideouſneſs. It is hardly poſſible to

ſee

ſee any thing in human ſhape more ugly, than one of theſe ſavages thus ſcarified, and farther ornamented with a fiſh bone ſtruck through the griſtle of the noſe. The cuſtom of daubing themſelves with white earth is alſo frequent among both ſexes: but, unlike the inhabitants of the iſlands in the Pacific Ocean, they reject the beautiful feathers which the birds of their country afford.

Excluſive of their weapons of offence, and a few ſtone hatchets very rudely faſhioned, their ingenuity is confined to manufacturing ſmall nets, in which they put the fiſh they catch, and to fiſh-hooks made of bone, neither of which are unſkilfully executed. On many of the rocks are alſo to be found delineations of the figures of men and birds, very poorly cut.

Of the uſe or benefit of cloathing, theſe people appear to have no comprehenſion, though their ſufferings from the climate they live in, ſtrongly point out the neceſſity of a covering from the rigour of the ſeaſons. Both

Both ſexes, and thoſe of all ages, are invariably found naked. But it muſt not be inferred from this, that cuſtom ſo inures them to the changes of the elements, as to make them bear with indifference the extremes of heat and cold; for we have had viſible and repeated proofs, that the latter affects them ſeverely, when they are ſeen ſhivering, and huddling themſelves up in heaps in their huts, or the caverns of the rocks, until a fire can be kindled.

Than theſe huts nothing more rude in conſtruction, or deficient in conveniency, can be imagined. They conſiſt only of pieces of bark laid together in the form of an oven, open at one end, and very low, though long enough for a man to lie at full length in. There is reaſon, however, to believe, that they depend leſs on them for ſhelter, than on the caverns with which the rocks abound.

To cultivation of the ground they are utter ſtrangers, and wholly depend for food on the few fruits they gather; the roots they dig

dig up in the ſwamps; and the fiſh they pick up along ſhore, or contrive to ſtrike from their canoes with ſpears. Fiſhing, indeed, ſeems to engroſs nearly the whole of their time, probably from its forming the chief part of a ſubſiſtence, which, obſervation has convinced us, nothing ſhort of the moſt painful labour, and unwearied aſſiduity can procure. When fiſh are ſcarce, which frequently happens, they often watch the moment of our hauling the ſeine, and have more than once been known to plunder its contents, in ſpite of the oppoſition of thoſe on the ſpot to guard it: and this even after having received a part of what had been caught. The only reſource at theſe times is to ſhew a muſquet, and if the bare ſight is not ſufficient, to fire it over their heads, which has ſeldom failed of diſperſing them hitherto, but how long the terror which it excites may continue is doubtful.

The canoes in which they fiſh are as deſpicable as their huts, being nothing more than a large piece of bark tied up at both ends with vines. Their dexterous management of them, added to the ſwiftneſs with which they paddle, and the boldneſs that leads them ſeveral miles in the open ſea, are, nevertheleſs, highly deſerving of admiration. A canoe is ſeldom ſeen without a fire in it, to dreſs the fiſh by, as ſoon as caught: fire they procure by attrition.

From their manner of diſpoſing of thoſe who die, which will be mentioned hereafter, as well as from every other obſervation, there ſeems no reaſon to ſuppoſe theſe people cannibals; nor do they ever eat animal ſubſtances in a raw ſtate, unleſs preſſed by extreme hunger, but indiſcriminately broil them, and their vegetables, on a fire, which renders theſe laſt an innocent food, though in their raw ſtate many of them are of a poiſonous quality: as a poor convict who unguardedly eat of them experienced, by falling a ſacrifice in twenty-four hours afterwards. If bread be given to the Indians, they chew and ſpit it out again, ſeldom chooſing to ſwallow it. Salt beef and pork they like rather better, but ſpirits they never could be brougnt to taſte a ſecond time.

The only domeſtic animal they have is the dog, which in their language is called Dingo, and a good deal reſembles the fox dog of England. Theſe animals are equally ſhy of us, and attached to the natives. One of them is now in the poſſeſſion of the Governor, and tolerably well reconciled to his new maſter. As the Indians ſee the diſlike of the dogs to us, they are ſometimes miſchievous enough to ſet them on ſingle perſons whom they chance to meet in the woods, A ſurly fellow was one day out ſhooting, when the natives attempted to divert themſelves in this manner at his expence. The man bore the teazing and gnawing of the dog at his heels for ſome time, but apprehending at length, that his patience might embolden them to uſe ſtill farther liberties, he turned round and ſhot poor Dingo dead on the ſpot: the owners of him ſet off with the utmoſt expedition.

There is no part of the behaviour of theſe people, that has puzzled us more, than that which relates to their women. Comparatively ſpeaking we have ſeen but few of them, and thoſe have been ſometimes kept back with every ſymptom of jealous ſenſibility; and ſometimes offered with every appearance of courteous familiarity. Cautious, however, of alarming the feelings of the men on ſo tender a point, we have conſtantly made a rule of treating the females with that diſtance and reſerve, which we judged moſt likely to remove any impreſſion they might have received of our intending ought, which could give offence on ſo delicate a ſubject. And ſo ſucceſsful have our endeavours been, that a quarrel on this head has in no inſtance, that I know of, happened. The tone of voice of the women, which is pleaſingly ſoft and feminine, forms a ſtriking contraſt to the rough guttural pronunciation of the men. Of the other charms of the ladies I ſhall be ſilent, though juſtice obliges me to mention, that, in the opinion of ſome amongſt us, they ſhew a degree of timidity and baſhfulneſs, which are, perhaps, inſeparable from the female character in its rudeſt ſtate. It is not a little ſingular, that the cuſtom of cutting off the two lower joints of the little finger of the left hand, obſerved in the Society Iſlands, is found here

here among the women, who have for the moſt part undergone this amputation. Hitherto we have not been able to trace out the cauſe of this uſage. At firſt we ſuppoſed it to be peculiar to the married women, or thoſe who had borne children; but this concluſion muſt have been erroneous, as we have no right to believe that celibacy prevails in any inſtance, and ſome of the oldeſt of the women are without this diſtinction; and girls of a very tender age are marked by it.

On firſt ſetting foot in the country, we were inclined to hold the ſpears of the natives very cheap. Fatal experience has, however, convinced us, that the wound inflicted by this weapon is not a trivial one; and that the ſkill of the Indians in throwing it, is far from deſpicable. Beſides more than a dozen convicts who have unaccountably diſappeared, we know that two, who were employed as ruſh cutters up the harbour, were (from what cauſe we are yet ignorant) moſt dreadfully mangled and butchered by the natives. A ſpear had paſſed entirely through

through the thickeſt part of the body of one of them, though a very robuſt man, and the ſkull of the other was beaten in. Their tools were taken away, but ſome proviſions which they had with them at the time of the murder, and their cloaths, were left untouched. In addition to this misfortune, two more convicts, who were peaceably engaged in picking of greens, on a ſpot very remote from that where their comrades ſuffered, were unawares attacked by a party of Indians, and before they could effect their eſcape, one of them was pierced by a ſpear in the hip, after which they knocked him down, and plundered his cloaths. The poor wretch, though dreadfully wounded, made ſhift to crawl off, but his companion was carried away by theſe barbarians, and his fate doubtful, until a ſoldier, a few days afterwards, picked up his jacket and hat in a native's hut, the latter pierced through by a ſpear. We have found that theſe ſpears are not made invariably alike, ſome of them being barbed like a fiſh gig, and others ſimply pointed. In repairing them they are no leſs dexterous than in throw-

throwing them. A broken one being given by a gentleman to an Indian, he inſtantly ſnatched up an oyſter-ſhell, and converted it with his teeth into a tool, with which he preſently faſhioned the ſpear, and rendered it fit for uſe: in performing this operation, the ſole of his foot ſerved him as a work-board. Nor are their weapons of offence confined to the ſpear only, for they have beſides long wooden ſwords, ſhaped like a ſabre, capable of inflicting a mortal wound, and clubs of an immenſe ſize. Small targets, made of the bark of trees, are likewiſe now and then to be ſeen among them.

From circumſtances which have been obſerved, we have ſometimes been inclined to believe theſe people at war with each other. They have more than once been ſeen aſſembled, as if bent on an expedition. An officer one day met fourteen of them marching along in a regular Indian file through the woods, each man armed with a ſpear in his right hand, and a large ſtone in his left: at their head appeared a chief, who was diſtinguiſhed by being painted. Though in the

pro-

proportion of five to one of our people they paſſed peaceably on.

That their ſkill in throwing the ſpear ſometimes enables them to kill the kangaroo we have no right to doubt, as a long ſplinter of this weapon was taken out of the thigh of one of theſe animals, over which the fleſh had completely cloſed; but we have never diſcovered that they have any method of enſnaring them, or that they know any other beaſts but the kangaroo and dog. Whatever animal is ſhewn them, a dog excepted, they call kangaroo: a ſtrong preſumption that the wild animals of the country are very few.

Soon after our arrival at Port Jackſon, I was walking out near a place where I obſerved a party of Indians, buſily employed in looking at ſome ſheep in an incloſure, and repeatedly crying out, Kangaroo, kangaroo! As this ſeemed to afford them pleaſure, I was willing to increaſe it by pointing out the horſes and cows, which were at no great diſtance. But unluckily, at the

moment,

moment, ſome female convicts, employed near the place, made their appearance, and all my endeavours to divert their attention from the ladies became fruitleſs. They attempted not, however, to offer them the leaſt degree of violence or injury, but ſtood at the diſtance of ſeveral paces, expreſſing very ſignificantly the manner they were attracted.

It would be treſpaſſing on the reader's indulgence were I to impoſe on him an account of any civil regulations, or ordinances, which may poſſibly exiſt among this people. I declare to him, that I know not of any, and that excepting a little tributary reſpect which the younger part appear to pay thoſe more advanced in years, I never could obſerve any degrees of ſubordination among them. To their religious rites and opinions I am equally a ſtranger. Had an opportunity offered of ſeeing the ceremonies obſerved at diſpoſing of the dead, perhaps, ſome inſight might have been gained; but all that we at preſent know with certainty is, that they burn the corpſe, and afterwards heap up the earth around it, ſomewhat in the manner of the ſmall tumuli, found in many counties of England.

I have already hinted, that the country is more populous than it was generally believed to be in Europe at the time of our ſailing. But this remark is not meant to be extended to the interior parts of the continent, which there is every reaſon to conclude from our reſearches, as well as from the manner of living practiſed by the natives, to be uninhabited. It appears as if ſome of the Indian families confine their ſociety and connections within their own pale: but that this cannot always be the caſe we know; for on the north-weſt arm of Botany Bay ſtands a village, which contains more than a dozen houſes, and perhaps five times that number of people; being the moſt conſiderable eſtabliſhment that we are acquainted with in the country. As a ſtriking proof, beſides, of the numerouſneſs of the natives, I beg leave to ſtate, that Governor Phillip, when on an excurſion between the head of this harbour and that of Botany Bay, once fell

in

in with a party, which confifted of more than three hundred perfons, two hundred and twelve of whom were men: this happened only on the day following the murder of the two convict rufh cutters, before noticed, and his Excellency was at the very time in fearch of the murderers, on whom, could they have been found, he intended to inflict a memorable and exemplary punifhment. The meeting was unexpected to both parties, and, confidering the critical fituation of affairs, perhaps not very pleafing to our fide, which confifted but of twelve perfons, until the peaceable difpofition of the Indians was manifeft. After the ftricteft fearch the Governor was obliged to return without having gained any information. The laudable perfeverance of his Excellency to throw every light on this unhappy and myfterious bufinefs did not, however, ftop here, for he inftituted the moft rigorous inquiry to find out, if poffible, whether the convicts had at any time ill treated or killed any of the natives; and farther, iffued a proclamation, offering the moft tempting of all rewards, a ftate of freedom, to him who

 fhould

ſhould point out the murderer, in caſe ſuch an one exiſted.

I have thus impartially ſtated the ſituation of matters, as they ſtand while I write, between the natives and us; that greater progreſs in attaching them to us has not been made, I have only to regret; but that all ranks of men have tried to effect it, by every reaſonable effort from which ſucceſs might have been expected, I can teſtify; nor can I omit ſaying, that in the higher ſtations this has been eminently conſpicuous. The public orders of Governor Phillip have invariably tended to promote ſuch a behaviour on our ſide, as was moſt likely to produce this much wiſhed-for event. To what cauſe then are we to attribute the diſtance which the accompliſhment of it appears at? I anſwer, to the fickle, jealous, wavering diſpoſition of the people we have to deal with, who, like all other ſavages, are either too indolent, too indifferent, or too fearful to form an attachment on eaſy terms, with thoſe who differ in habits and manners ſo widely from themſelves. Before I cloſe the ſubject, I cannot, however,

ever, omit to relate the following ludicrous adventure, which poſſibly may be of greater uſe in effecting what we have ſo much at heart, than all our endeavours.

Some young gentlemen belonging to the Sirius one day met a native, an old man, in the woods; he had a beard conſiderable length, which his new acquaintance gave him to underſtand, by ſignals, they would rid him of, if he pleaſed; ſtroaking their chins, and ſhewing him the ſmoothneſs of them at the ſame time; at length the old Indian conſented, and one of the young-ſters taking a penknife from his pocket, and making uſe of the beſt ſubſtitute for lather he could find, performed the operation with great ſucceſs, and, as it proved, much to the liking of the old man, who in a few days after repoſed a confidence in us, of which we had hitherto known no example, by pad-dling along-ſide the Sirius in his canoe, and pointing to his beard. Various arts were ineffectually tried to induce him to enter the ſhip; but as he continued to decline the invitation, a barber was ſent down into the

the boat along-ſide the canoe, from whence, leaning over the gunnel, he complied with the wiſh of the old beau, to his infinite ſatisfaction. In addition to the conſequences which our ſanguine hopes led us to expect from this dawning of cordiality, it affords proof, that the beard is conſidered by this people more as an incumbrance than a mark of dignity.

CHAP.

CHAP. XII.

The Departure of the French from Botany Bay; *and the Return of the* Supply *from* Norfolk Iſland; *with a Diſcovery made by Lieutenant* Ball *on his Paſſage to it.*

March 1788.

ABOUT the middle of the month our good friends the French departed from Botany Bay, in proſecution of their voyage. During their ſtay in that port the officers of the two nations had frequent opportunities of teſtifying their mutual regard by viſits, and every interchange of friendſhip and eſteem. Theſe ſhips ſailed from France, by order of the King, on the 1ſt of Auguſt, 1785, under the command of Monſieur De Perrouſe, an officer whoſe eminent qualifications, we had reaſon to think, entitle him to fill the higheſt ſtations. In England particularly, he ought long to be remembered with admiration and gratitude, for the humanity which marked his conduct, when ordered to deſtroy our ſettlement at Hudſon's Bay, in the laſt war. His ſecond in command was the Chevalier Clonard, an officer alſo of diſtinguiſhed merit.

In the courſe of the voyage theſe ſhips had been ſo unfortunate as to loſe a boat, with many men and officers in her, off the weſt of California; and afterwards met with an accident ſtill more to be regretted, at an iſland in the Pacific Ocean, diſcovered by Monſieur Bougainville, in the latitude of 14° 19′ ſouth, longitude 173° 3′ 20″ eaſt of Paris. Here they had the misfortune to have no leſs than thirteen of their crews, among whom was the officer at that time ſecond in command, cut off by the natives, and many more deſperately wounded. To what cauſe this cruel event was to be attributed, they knew not, as they were about to quit the iſland after having lived with the Indians in the greateſt harmony for ſeveral weeks; and exchanged, during the time, their European commodities for the produce of the place, which they deſcribe as filled with a race of people remarkable for beauty and

and comelineſs; and abounding in refreſhments of all kinds.

It was no leſs gratifying to an Engliſh ear, than honourable to Monſieur De Perrouſe, to witneſs the feeling manner in which he always mentioned the name and talents of Captain Cook. That illuſtrious circumnavigator had, he ſaid, left nothing to thoſe who might follow in his track to deſcribe, or fill up. As I found, in the courſe of converſation, that the French ſhips had touched at the Sandwich Iſlands, I aſked M. De Perrouſe what reception he had met with there. His anſwer deſerves to be known: "During the whole of our voyage "in the South Seas, the people of the Sand-"wich Iſlands were the only Indians who "never gave us cauſe of complaint. They "furniſhed us liberally with proviſions, and "adminiſtered cheerfully to all our wants." It may not be improper to remark, that Owhyee was not one of the iſlands viſited by this gentleman.

In the ſhort ſtay made by theſe ſhips at Botany Bay, an Abbé, one of the naturaliſts on board, died, and was buried on the north ſhore. The French had hardly departed, when the natives pulled down a ſmall board, which had been placed over the ſpot where the corpſe was interred, and defaced every thing around. On being informed of it, the Governor ſent a party over with orders to affix a plate of copper on a tree near the place, with the following inſcription on it, which is a copy of what was written on the board:

Hic jacet L. RECEVEUR,

E. F. F. minnibus Galliæ, Sacerdos, Phyſicus, in circumnavigatione mundi, Duce De La Perrouſe.

Obiit die 17° Februarii, anno 1788.

This mark of reſpectful attention was more particularly due, from M. De Perrouſe having, when at Kamſchatka, paid a ſimilar tribute of gratitude to the memory of Captain

Captain Clarke, whoſe tomb was found in nearly as ruinous a ſtate as that of the Abbé.

Like ourſelves, the French found it neceſſary, more than once, to chaſtiſe a ſpirit of rapine and intruſion which prevailed among the Indians around the Bay. The menace of pointing a muſquet to them was frequently uſed; and in one or two inſtances it was fired off, though without being attended with fatal conſequences. Indeed the French commandant, both from a regard to the orders of his Court, as well as to our quiet and ſecurity, ſhewed a moderation and forbearance on this head highly becoming.

On the 20th of March, the Supply arrived from Norfolk Iſland, after having ſafely landed Lieutenant King and his little garriſon. The pine-trees growing there are deſcribed to be of a growth and height ſuperior, perhaps, to any in the world. But the difficulty of bringing them away will not be eaſily ſurmounted from the badneſs and danger of the landing place. After the moſt exact ſearch, not a ſingle plant of the New

Zealand flax could be found, though we had been taught to believe it abounded there.

Lieutenant Ball, in returning to Port Jackſon, touched at a ſmall iſland in latitude 31° 36′ ſouth, longitude 159° 4′ eaſt of Greenwich, which he had been fortunate enough to diſcover on his paſſage to Norfolk, and to which he gave the name of Lord Howe's Iſland. It is entirely without inhabitants, or any traces of any having ever been there. But it happily abounds in what will be infinitely more importance to the ſettlers on New South Wales: green turtle of the fineſt kind frequent it in the ſummer ſeaſon. Of this Mr. Ball gave us ſome very handſome and acceptable ſpecimens on his return. Beſides turtle, the iſland is well ſtocked with birds, many of them ſo tame as to be knocked down by the ſeamen with ſticks. At the diſtance of four leagues from Lord Howe's Iſland, and in latitude 31° 30 ſouth, longitude 159° 8 eaſt, ſtands a remarkable rock, of conſiderable height, to which Mr. Ball gave the name of Ball's Pyramid, from the ſhape it bears.

While

While the Supply was abſent, Governor Phillip made an excurſion to Broken Bay, a few leagues to the northward of Port Jackſon, in order to explore it. As a harbour it almoſt equals the latter, but the adjacent country was found ſo rocky and bare, as to preclude all poſſibility of turning it to account. Some rivulets of freſh water fall into the head of the Bay, forming a very pictureſque ſcene. The Indians who live on its banks are numerous, and behaved attentively in a variety of inſtances while our people remained among them.

CHAP.

CHAP. XIII.

Tranſactions at Port Jackſon, *in the Months of* April *and* May.

April, 1788.

AS winter was faſt approaching, it became neceſſary to ſecure ourſelves in quarters, which might ſhield us from the cold we were taught to expect in this hemiſphere, though in ſo low a latitude. The erection of barracks for the ſoldiers was projected, and the private men of each company undertook to build for themſelves two wooden houſes, of ſixty-eight feet in length, and twenty-three in breadth. To forward the deſign, ſeveral ſaw-pits were immediately ſet to work, and four ſhip carpenters attached to the battalion, for the purpoſe of directing and completing this neceſſary undertaking. In proſecuting it, however, ſo many difficulties occurred, that we were ſeign to circumſcribe our original intentions; and, inſtead of eight houſes, content ourſelves with four. And even theſe, from the badneſs of the timber, the ſcarcity of artificers, and other impediments, are at the day on which I write, ſo little advanced, that it will be well, if at the cloſe of the year 1788, we ſhall be eſtabliſhed in them. In the mean while the married people, by proceeding on a more contracted ſcale, were ſoon under comfortable ſhelter. Nor were the convicts forgotten; and as leiſure was frequently afforded them for the purpoſe, little edifices quickly multiplied on the ground allotted them to build upon.

But as theſe habitations were intended by Governor Phillip, to anſwer only the exigency of the moment, the plan of a town was drawn, and the ground on which it is hereafter to ſtand ſurveyed, and marked out. To proceed on a narrow, confined ſcale, in a country of the extenſive limits we poſſeſs, would be unpardonable: extent of empire demands grandeur of deſign. That this has been our view will be readily believed, when I tell the reader, that the principal ſtreet in our projected city will be, when completed,

agreeable

agreeable to the plan laid down, two hundred feet in breadth, and all the reſt of a correſponding proportion. How far this will be accompanied with adequate diſpatch, is another queſtion, as the incredulous among us are ſometimes hardy enough to declare, that ten times our ſtrength would not be able to finiſh it in as many years.

Invariably intent on exploring a country, from which curioſity promiſes ſo many gratifications, his Excellency about this time undertook an expedition into the interior parts of the continent. His party conſiſted of eleven perſons, who, after being conveyed by water to the head of the harbour, proceeded in a weſterly direction, to reach a chain of mountains, which in clear weather are diſcernible, though at an immenſe diſtance, from ſome heights near our encampment. With unwearied induſtry they continued to penetrate the country for four days; but at the end of that time, finding the baſe of the mountain to be yet at the diſtance of more than twenty miles, and proviſions growing ſcarce, it was judged prudent

prudent to return, without having accomplifhed the end for which the expedition had been undertaken. To reward their toils, our adventurers had, however, the pleafure of difcovering and traverfing an extenfive tract of ground, which they had reafon to believe, from the obfervations they were enabled to make, capable of producing every thing, which a happy foil and genial climate can bring forth. In addition to this flattering appearance, the face of the country is fuch, as to promife fuccefs whenever it fhall be cultivated, the trees being at a confiderable diftance from each other, and the intermediate fpace filled, not with underwood, but a thick rich grafs, growing in the utmoft luxuriancy. I muft not, however, conceal, that in this long march, our gentlemen found not a fingle rivulet, but were under a neceffity of fupplying themfelves with water from ftanding pools, which they met with in the vallies, fuppofed to be formed by the rains that fall at particular feafons of the year. Nor had they the good fortune to fee any quadrupeds worth notice, except a few kangaroos. To their great furprize, they obſerved indiſputable tracks of the natives having been lately there, though in their whole route none of them were to be ſeen; nor any means to be traced, by which they could procure ſubſiſtence ſo far from the ſea ſhore.

On the 6th of May the Supply ſailed for Lord Howe Iſland, to take on board turtle for the ſettlement; but after waiting there ſeveral days was obliged to return without having ſeen one, owing we apprehended to the advanced ſeaſon of the year. Three of the tranſports alſo, which were engaged by the Eaſt India Company to proceed to China, to take on board a lading of tea, ſailed about this time for Canton.

The unſucceſsful return of the Supply caſt a general damp on our ſpirits, for by this time freſh proviſions were become ſcarcer than in a blockaded town. The little live ſtock, which with ſo heavy an expence, and through ſo many difficulties, we had brought on ſhore, prudence forbade us to uſe; and fiſh, which on our arrival, and

for

for a ſhort time after had been tolerable plenty, were become ſo ſcarce, as to be rarely ſeen at the tables of the firſt among us. Had it not been for a ſtray kangaroo, which fortune now and then threw in our way, we ſhould have been utter ſtrangers to the taſte of freſh food.

Thus ſituated, the ſcurvy began its uſual ravages, and extended its baneful influence, more or leſs, through all deſcriptions of perſons. Unfortunately the eſculent vegetable productions of the country are neither plentiful, nor tend very effectually to remove this diſeaſe. And the ground we had turned up and planted with garden ſeeds, either from the nature of the ſoil, or, which is more probable, the lateneſs of the ſeaſon, yielded but a ſcanty and inſufficient ſupply of what we ſtood ſo greatly in need of.

During the period I am deſcribing, few enormous offences were perpetrated by the convicts. A petty theft was now and then heard of, and a ſpirit of refractory ſullenneſs broke out at times in ſome individuals: one execution only, however, took place. The ſufferer, who was a very young man, was convicted of a burglary, and met his fate with a hardineſs and inſenſibility, which the groſſeſt ignorance, and moſt deplorable want of feeling, alone could ſupply.

CHAP. XIV.

From the Beginning of June, *to the Departure of the Ships for* Europe.

HOURS of feſtivity, which under happier ſkies paſs away unregarded, and are ſoon conſigned to oblivion, acquire in this forlorn and diſtant circle a ſuperior degree of acceptable importance,

On the anniverſary of the King's birthday all the officers not on duty, both of the garriſon and his Majeſty's ſhips, dined with the Governor. On ſo joyful an occaſion, the firſt too ever celebrated in our new ſettlement, it were needleſs to ſay, that loyal conviviality dictated every ſentiment, and inſpired every gueſt. Among other public toaſts drunk, was, proſperity to Sydney Cove, in Cumberland county, now named ſo by authority. At daylight in the morning the ſhips of war had fired twenty-one guns each, which was repeated at noon, and

and anſwered by three vollies from the battalion of marines.

Nor were the officers alone partakers of the general relaxation. The four unhappy wretches labouring under ſentence of baniſhment were freed from their fetters, to rejoin their former ſociety; and three days given as holidays to every convict in the colony. Hoſpitality too, which ever acquires a double reliſh by being extended, was not forgotten on the 4th of June, when each priſoner, male and female, received an allowance of grog; and every non-commiſſioned officer and private ſoldier had the honor of drinking proſperity to his royal maſter, in a pint of porter, ſerved out at the flag ſtaff, in addition to the cuſtomary allowance of ſpirits. Bonfires concluded the evening, and I am happy to ſay, that excepting a ſingle inſtance which ſhall be taken notice of hereafter, no bad conſequence, or unpleaſant remembrance, flowed from an indulgence ſo amply beſtowed.

About this time [June] an accident happened, which I record with much regret. The whole of our black cattle, consisting of five cows and a bull, either from not being properly secured, or from the negligence of those appointed to take care of them, strayed into the woods, and in spite of all the search we have been able to make, are not yet found. As a convict of the name of Corbet, who was accused of a theft, eloped nearly at the same time, it was at first believed, that he had taken the desperate measure of driving off the cattle, in order to subsist on them as long as possible; or perhaps to deliver them to the natives. In this uncertainty, parties to search were sent out in different directions; and the fugitive declared an outlaw, in case of not returning by a fixed day. After much anxiety and fatigue, those who had undertaken the task returned without finding the cattle. But on the 21st of the month, Corbet made his appearance, near a farm belonging to the Governor, and entreated a convict, who happened to be on the spot, to give him some food, as he was perishing for hunger. The man applied to,

under

under pretence of fetching what he aſked for, went away and immediately gave the neceſſary information, in conſequence of which a party under arms was ſent out and apprehended him. When the poor wretch was brought in, he was greatly emaciated and almoſt famiſhed. But on proper reſtoratives being adminiſtered, he was ſo far recovered by the 24th, as to be able to ſtand his trial, when he pleaded Guilty to the robbery with which he ſtood charged, and received ſentence of death In the courſe of repeated examinations it plainly appeared, he was an utter ſtranger to the place where the cattle might be, and was in no ſhape concerned in having driven them off.

Samuel Peyton, convict, for having on the evening of the King's birth-day broke open an officer's marquee, with an intent to commit robbery, of which he was fully convicted, had ſentence of death paſſed on him at the ſame time as Corbet; and on the following day they were both executed; confeſſing the juſtneſs of their fate, and imploring the forgiveneſs of thoſe whom they

had

had injured. Peyton, at the time of his ſuffering, was but twenty years of age, the greateſt part of which had been invariably paſſed in the commiſſion of crimes, that at length terminated in his ignominious end. The following letter, written by a fellow convict to the ſufferer's unhappy mother, I ſhall make no apology for preſenting to the reader; it affords a melancholy proof, that not the ignorant and untaught only have provoked the juſtice of their country to baniſh them to this remote region.

"Sydney Cove, Port Jackſon,
New South Wales, 24th June, 1788.

"My dear and honoured mother!

"WITH a heart oppreſſed by the keeneſt ſenſe of anguiſh, and too much agitated by the idea of my very melancholy condition, to expreſs my own ſentiments, I have prevailed on the goodneſs of a commiſerating friend, to do me the laſt ſad office of acquainting you with the dreadful fate that awaits me.

" My dear mother! with what agony of ſoul do I dedicate the few laſt moments of my life, to bid you an eternal adieu: my doom being irrevocably fixed, and ere this hour to-morrow I ſhall have quitted this vale of wretchedneſs, to enter into an unknown and endleſs eternity. I will not diſtreſs your tender maternal feelings by any long comment on the cauſe of my preſent misfortune. Let it therefore ſuffice to ſay, that impelled by that ſtrong propenſity to evil, which neither the virtuous precepts nor example of the beſt of parents could eradicate, I have at length fallen an unhappy, though juſt, victim to my own follies.

" Too late I regret my inattention to your admonitions, and feel myſelf ſenſibly affected by the remembrance of the many anxious moments you have paſſed on my account. For theſe, and all my other tranſgreſſions, however great, I ſupplicate the Divine forgiveneſs; and encouraged by the promiſes of that Saviour who died for us all, I truſt to receive that mercy in the world to

come,

come, which my offences have deprived me of all hope, or expectation of, in this. The affliction which this will cost you, I hope the Almighty will enable you to bear. Banish from your memory all my former indiscretions, and let the cheering hope of a happy meeting hereafter, console you for my loss. Sincerely penitent for my sins; sensible of the justice of my conviction and sentence, and firmly relying on the merits of a Blessed Redeemer, I am at perfect peace with all mankind, and trust I shall yet experience that peace, which this world cannot give. Commend my soul to the Divine mercy. I bid you an eternal farewell.

Your unhappy dying Son,

SAMUEL PEYTON."

"To Mrs. Peyton,
London."

After this nothing occurred with which I think it necessary to trouble the reader. The contents of the following chapters could not, I conceive, be so properly interwoven in the body of the work; I have, therefore, assigned them a place by themſelves, with a view that the concluſions adopted in them may be more ſtrongly enforced on the minds of thoſe, to whom they are more particularly addreſſed

CHAP.

C H A P. XV.

The Face of the Country; its Productions, Climate, &c.

TO the geographical knowledge of this country, ſupplied by Captain Cook, and Captain Furneaux, we are able to add nothing. The latter explored the coaſt from Van Dieman's land to the latitude of 39° ſouth; and Cook from Point Hicks, which lies in 37° 58, to Endeavour Streights. The intermediate ſpace between the end of Furneaux's diſcovery and Point Hicks, is, therefore, the only part of the ſouth-eaſt coaſt unknown, and it ſo happened on our paſſage thither, owing to the weather, which forebade any part of the ſhips engaging with the ſhore, that we are unable to pronounce whether, or not, a ſtraight interſects the continent hereabouts: though I beg leave to ſay, that I have been informed by a naval friend, that when the fleet was off this part of the coaſt, a ſtrong ſet-off ſhore was plainly felt.

At the diſtance of 60 miles inland, a prodigious chain of lofty mountains runs nearly in a north and ſouth direction, further than the eye can trace them. Should nothing intervene to prevent it, the Governor intends, ſhortly, to explore their ſummits: and, I think there can be little doubt, that his curioſity will not go unrewarded. If large rivers do exiſt in the country, which ſome of us are almoſt ſceptical enough to doubt, their ſources muſt ariſe amidſt theſe hills; and the direction they run in, for a conſiderable diſtance, muſt be either due north, or due ſouth. For it is ſtrikingly ſingular that three ſuch noble harbours as Botany Bay, Port Jackſon, and Broken Bay, alike end in ſhallows and ſwamps, filled with mangroves.

The general face of the country is certainly pleaſing, being diverſified with gentle aſcents, and little winding vallies, covered for the moſt part with large ſpreading trees, which

which afford a succession of leaves in all seasons. In those places where trees are scarce, a variety of flowering shrubs abound, most of them entirely new to an European, and surpassing in beauty, fragrance, and number, all I ever saw in an uncultivated state: among these, a tall shrub, bearing an elegant white flower, which smells like English May, is particularly delightful, and perfumes the air around to a great distance. The species of trees are few, and, I am concerned to add, the wood universally of so bad a grain, as almost to preclude a possibility of using it a the increase of labour occasioned by this in our buildings has been such, as nearly to exceed belief. These trees yield a profusion of thick red gum (not unlike the sanguis draconis) which is found serviceable in medicine, particularly in dysenteric complaints, where it has sometimes succeeded, when all other preparations have failed. To blunt its acrid qualities, it is usual to combine it with opiates.

The nature of the ſoil is various. That immediately round Sydney Cove is ſandy, with here and there a ſtratum of clay. From the ſand we have yet been able to draw very little; but there ſeems no reaſon to doubt, that many large tracts of land around us will bring to perfection whatever ſhall be ſown in them. To give this matter a fair trial, ſome practical farmers capable of ſuch an undertaking ſhould be ſent out; for the ſpots we have choſen for experiments in agriculture, in which we can ſcarce be ſuppoſed adepts, have hitherto but ill repaid our toil, which may be imputable to our having choſen ſuch as are unfavourable for our purpoſe.

Except from the ſize of the trees, the difficulties of clearing the land are not numerous, underwood being rarely found, though the country is not abſolutely without it. Of the natural meadows which Mr Cook mentions near Botany Bay, we can give no account; none ſuch exiſt about Port Jackſon. Graſs, however, grows in every place but the ſwamps with the greateſt vigour and luxu-

luxuriancy, though it is not of the fineſt quality, and is found to agree better with horſes and cows than ſheep. A few wild fruits are ſometimes procured, among which is the ſmall purple apple mentioned by Cook, and a fruit which has the appearance of a grape, though in taſte more like a green gooſberry, being exceſſively ſour: probably were it meliorated by cultivation, it would become more palatable.

Freſh water, as I have ſaid before, is found but in inconſiderable quantities. For the common purpoſes of life there is gene rally enough; but we know of no ſtream in the country capable of turning a mill: and the remark made by Mr. Anderſon, of the dryneſs of the country round Adventure Bay, extends without exception to every part of it which we have penetrated.

Previous to leaving England I remember to have frequently heard it aſſerted, that the diſcovery of mines was one of the ſecondary objects of the expedition. Perhaps there are mines; but as no perſon competent to form a decifion is to be found among us, I wifh no one to adopt an idea, that I mean to imprefs him with fuch a belief, when I ftate, that individuals, whofe judgements are not defpicable, are willing to think favourably of this conjecture, from fpecimens of ore feen in many of the ftones picked up here. I cannot quit this fubject without regretting, that fome one capable of throwing a better light on it, is not in the colony. Nor can I help being equally concerned, that an experienced botanift was not fent out, for the purpofe of collecting and defcribing the rare and beautiful plants with which the country abounds. Indeed, we flattered ourfelves, when at the Cape of Good Hope, that Mafon, the King's botanical gardener, who was employed there in collecting for the royal nurfery at Kew, would have joined us, but it feems his orders and engagements prevented him from quitting that beaten track, to enter on this fcene of novelty and variety.

To the naturalift this country holds out many invitations.—Birds, though not remarkably

markably numerous, are in great variety, and of the moſt exquiſite beauty of plumage, among which are the cockatoo lo ry, and parroquet: but the bird which principally claims attention is, a ſpecies of oſtrich, approaching nearer to the emu of South America than any other we know of. One of them was ſhot, at a conſiderable diſtance, with a ſingle ball, by a convict employed for that purpoſe by the Governor; its weight, when complete, was ſeventy pounds, and its length from the end of the toe to the tip of the beak, ſeven feet two inches, though there was reaſon to believe it had not attained its full growth. On diſſection many anatomical ſingularities were obſerved the gall-bladder was remarkably large, the liver not bigger than that of a barn-door fowl, and after the ſtricteſt ſearch no gizzard could be found; the legs, which were of a vaſt length, were covered with thick ſtrong ſcales, plainly indicating the animal to be formed for living amidſt deſarts; and the foot differed from an oſtrich's by forming a triangle inſtead of being cloven. Goldſmith, whoſe account of the emu is the only one I can refer to, ſays, " that it is covered from the back and rump with long feathers, which fall back ward, and cover the anus; theſe feathers are grey on the back, and white on the belly." The wings are ſo ſmall as hardly to deſerve the name, and are unfurniſhed with thoſe beautiful ornaments which adorn the wings of the oſtrich: all the feathers are extremely coarſe, but the conſtruction of them deſerves notice—they grow in pairs from a ſingle ſhaft, a ſingularity which the author I have quoted has omitted to remark. It may be preſumed, that theſe birds are not very ſcarce, as ſeveral have been ſeen, ſome of them immenſely large but they are ſo wild, as to make ſhooting them a matter of great difficulty. Though incapable of flying, they run with ſuch ſwiftneſs, that our fleeteſt greyhounds are left far behind in every attempt to catch them. The fleſh was eaten, and taſted like beef.

Beſides the emu, many birds of prodigious ſize have been ſeen, which promiſe to increaſe the number of thoſe deſcribed by naturaliſts, whenever we ſhall be fortunate enough to obtain them; but among theſe the bat of the Endeavour river is not to be found. In the woods are various little ſongſters, whoſe notes are equally ſweet and plaintive.

Of quadrupeds, except the kangaroo, I have little to ſay. The few met with are almoſt invariably of the opoſſum tribe, but even theſe do not abound. To beaſts of prey we are utter ſtrangers, nor have we yet any cauſe to believe that they exiſt in the counry. And happy it is for us that they do not, as their preſence would deprive us of the only freſh meals the ſettlement affords, the fleſh of the kangaroo. This ſingular animal is already known in Europe by the drawing and deſcription of Mr. Cook. To the drawing nothing can be objected but the poſition of the claws of the hinder leg, which are mixed together like thoſe of a dog, whereas no ſuch indiſtinctneſs is to be found in the animal I am deſcribing. It was the Chevalier

lier De Perrouſe who pointed out this to me, while we were comparing a kangaroo with the plate, which, as he juſtly obſerved, is correct enough to give the world in general a good idea of the animal, but not ſufficiently accurate for the man of ſcience

Of the natural hiſtory of the kangaroo we are ſtill very ignorant. We may, however, venture to pronounce this animal, a new ſpecies of opoſſum, the female being furniſhed with a bag, in which the young is contained; and in which the teats are found. Theſe laſt are only two in number, a ſtrong preſumptive proof, had we no other evidence, that the kangaroo brings forth rarely more than one at a birth. But this is ſettled beyond a doubt, from more than a dozen females having been killed, which had invariably but one formed in the pouch. Notwithſtanding this, the animal may be looked on as prolific, from the early age it begins to breed at, kangaroos with young having been taken of not more than thirty pounds weight; and there is room to believe that when at their utmoſt growth, they weigh not

not lefs than one hundred and fifty pounds. A male of one hundred and thirty pounds weight has been killed, whofe dimenfions were as follows:

	Ft.	Inch.
Extreme length — —	7	3
Do. of the tail — —	3	4½
Do. of the hinder legs —	3	2
Do. of the fore paws — —	1	7½
Circumference of the tail of the root. — — — —	1	5

After this perhaps I fhall hardly be credited, when I affirm that the kangaroo on being brought forth is not larger than an Englifh moufe. It is, however, in my power to fpeak pofitively on this head, as I have feen more than one inftance of it.

In running, this animal confines himfelf entirely to his hinder legs, which are poffeffed with an extraordinary mufcular power. Their fpeed is very great, though not in general quite equal to that of a greyhound; but when the greyhounds are fo fortunate as to

feize

ſeize them, they are incapable of retaining their hold, from the amazing ſtruggles of the animal. The bound of the kangaroo, when not hard preſſed, has been meaſured, and found to exceed twenty feet.

At what time of the year they copulate, and in what manner, we know not: the teſticles of the male are placed contrary to the uſual order of nature.

When young, the kangaroo eats tender and well flavoured, taſting like veal, but the old ones are more tough and ſtringy than bull-beef. They are not carnivorous, and ſubſiſt altogether on particular flowers and graſs. Their bleat is mournful, and very different from that of any other animal, it is, however, ſeldom heard but in the young-ones.

Fiſh, which our ſanguine hopes led us to expect in great quantities, do not abound. In ſummer they are tolerably plentiful, but for ſome months paſt very few have been taken. Botany Bay in this reſpect exceeds Port

Port Jackſon The French once caught near two thouſand fiſh in one day, of a ſpecies of grouper, to which, from the form of a bone in the head reſembling a helmet, we have given the name of light horſeman. To this may be added baſs, mullets, ſkait, ſoles, leather-jackets, and many other ſpecies, all ſo good in their kind, as to double our regret at their not being more numerous. Sharks of an enormous ſize are found here. One of theſe was caught by the people on board the Sirius, which meaſured at the ſhoulders ſix feet and a half in circumference. His liver yielded twenty-four gallons of oil; and in his ſtomach was found the head of a ſhark, which had been thrown overboard from the ſame ſhip. The Indians, probably from having felt the effects of their voracious fury, teſtify the utmoſt horror on ſeeing theſe terrible fiſh.

Venomous animals and reptiles are rarely ſeen. Large ſnakes beautifully variegated have been killed, but of the effect of their bites we are happily ignorant. Inſects, though numerous, are by no means, even in ſummer, ſo troubleſome as I have found them in America, the Weſt Indies, and other countries.

The climate is undoubtedly very deſirable to live in. In ſummer the heats are uſually moderated by the ſea breeze, which ſets in early; and in winter the degree of cold is ſo ſlight as to occaſion no inconvenience; once or twice we have had hoar froſts and hail, but no appearance of ſnow The thermometer has never riſen beyond 84, nor fallen lower than 35, in general it ſtood in the beginning of February at between 78 and 74 at noon. Nor is the temperature of the air leſs healthy than pleaſant. Thoſe dreadful putrid fevers by which new countries are ſo often ravaged, are unknown to us; and excepting a ſlight diarrhœa, which prevailed ſoon after we had landed, and was fatal in very few inſtances, we are ſtrangers to epidemic diſeaſes.

On the whole, (thunder ſtorms in the hot months excepted) I know not any climate equal to this I write in. Ere we had been a fort-

fortnight on ſhore we experienced ſome ſtorms of thunder accompanied with rain, than which nothing can be conceived more violent and tremendous, and their repetition for ſeveral days, joined to the damage they did, by killing ſeveral of our ſheep, led us to draw preſages of an unpleaſant nature Happily, however, for many months we have eſcaped any ſimiliar viſitations.

CHAP. XVI.

The Progreſs made in the Settlement; and the Situation of Affairs at the Time of the Ship, which conveys this Account, ſailing for England.

FOR the purpoſe of expediting the public work, the male convicts have been divided into gangs, over each of which a perſon, ſelected from among themſelves, is placed. It is to be regretted that Government did not take this matter into conſideration before we left England, and appoint proper perſons with reaſonable ſalaries to execute the office of overſeers; as the conſequence of our preſent imperfect plan is ſuch, as to defeat in a great meaſure the purpoſes for which the priſoners were ſent out. The female convicts have hitherto lived in a ſtate of total idleneſs; except a few who are kept at work in making pegs for tiles, and picking up ſhells for burning into lime. For the laſt

time

time I repeat, that the behaviour of all claſſes of theſe people ſince our arrival in the ſettlement has been better than could, I think, have been expected from them.

Temporary wooden ſtorehouſes covered with thatch or ſhingles, in which the cargoes of all the ſhips have been lodged, are completed; and an hoſpital is erected. Barracks for the military are conſiderably advanced; and little huts to ſerve, until ſomething more permanent can be finiſhed, have been raiſed on all ſides. Notwithſtanding this the encampments of the marines and convicts are ſtill kept up; and to ſecure their owners from the coldneſs of the nights, are covered in with buſhes, and thatched over.

The plan of a town I have already ſaid is marked out. And as free-ſtone of an excellent quality abounds, one requiſite towards the completion of it is attained. Only two houſes of ſtone are yet begun, which are intended for the Governor and Lieutenant Governor. One of the greateſt impediments we meet with, is a want of limeſtone, of which

which no ſigns appear. Clay for making bricks is in plenty, and a conſiderable quantity of them burned and ready for uſe.

In enumerating the public buildings I find I have been ſo remiſs as to omit an obſervatory, which is erected at a ſmall diſtance from the encampments. It is nearly completed, and when fitted up with the teleſcopes and other aſtronomical inſtruments ſent out by the Board of Longitude, will afford a deſirable retreat from the liſtleſſneſs of a camp evening at Port Jackſon. One of the principal reaſons which induced the Board to grant this apparatus was, for the purpoſe of enabling Lieutenant Dawes of the marines, (to whoſe care it is intruſted) to make obſervations on a comet which is ſhortly expected to appear in the ſouthern hemiſphere. The latitude of the obſervatory, from the reſult of more than three hundred obſervations, is fixed at 33° 52′ 30″ ſouth, and the longitude at 151° 16′ 30″ eaſt of Greenwich. The latitude of the ſouth head which forms the entrance of the harbour, 33° 51′, and that of the

the north head oppoſite to it at 33° 49′ 45″ ſouth.

Since landing here our military force has ſuffered a diminution of only three perſons, a ſerjeant and two privates. Of the convicts fifty-four have periſhed, including the executions. Amidſt the cauſes of this mortality, exceſſive toil and a ſcarcity of food are not to be numbered, as the reader will eaſily conceive, when informed, that they have the ſame allowance of proviſions as every officer and ſoldier in the garriſon; and are indulged by being exempted from labour every Saturday afternoon and Sunday. On the latter of thoſe days they are expected to attend divine ſervice, which is performed either within one of the ſtorehouſes, or under a great tree in the open air, until a church can be built.

Amidſt our public labours, that no fortified poſt, or place of ſecurity, is yet begun, may be a matter of ſurpriſe. Were an emergency in the night to happen, it is not eaſy to ſay what might not take place before troops

troops, ſcattered about in an extenſive en campment, could be formed, ſo as to act. An event that happened a few evenings ſince may, perhaps, be the means of forwarding this neceſſary work. In the dead of night the centinels on the eaſtern ſide of the cove were alarmed by the voices of the Indians, talking near their poſts. The ſoldiers on this occaſion acted with their uſual firmneſs, and without creating a diſturbance, acquainted the officer of the guard with the circumſtance, who immediately took every precaution to prevent an attack, and at the ſame time gave orders that no moleſtation, while they continued peaceable, ſhould be offered them. From the darkneſs of the night, and the diſtance they kept at, it was not eaſy to aſcertain their number, but from the ſound of the voices and other circumſtances, it was calculated at near thirty. To their intentions in honouring us with this viſit (the only one we have had from them in the laſt five months) we are ſtrangers, though moſt probably it was either with a view to pilfer, or to aſcertain in what ſecurity we ſlept, and the precautions we uſed

in

in the night. When the bells of the ſhips in the harbour ſtruck the hour of the night, and the centinels called out on their poſts "All's well," they obſerved a dead ſilence, and continued it for ſome minutes, though talking with the greateſt earneſtneſs and vociferation but the moment before. After having remained a conſiderable time they departed without interchanging a ſyllable with our people.

CHAP. XVII.

Some Thoughts on the Advantages which may arise to the Mother Country from forming the Colony.

THE author of these sheets would subject himself to the charge of presumption, were he to aim at developing the intentions of Government in forming this settlement. But without giving offence, or incurring reproach, he hopes his opinion on the probability of advantage to be drawn from hence by Great Britain, may be fairly made known.

If only a receptacle for convicts be intended, this place stands unequalled from the situation, extent, and nature of the country. When viewed in a commercial light, I fear its insignificance will appear very striking. The New Zealand hemp, of which so many sanguine expectations

were

were formed, is not a native of the ſoil; and Norfolk Iſland, where we made ſure to find this article, is alſo without it. So that the ſcheme of being able to aſſiſt the Eaſt Indies with naval ſtores, in caſe of a war, muſt fall to the ground, both from this deficiency, and the quality of the timber growing here. Were it indeed poſſible to tranſport that of Norfolk Iſland, its value would be found very great, but the difficulty, from the ſurf, I am well informed, is ſo inſuperable as to forbid the attempt. Lord Howe Iſland, diſcovered by Lieut. Ball, though an ineſtimable acquiſition to our colony, produces little elſe than the mountain cabbage tree.

Should a ſufficient military force be ſent out to thoſe employed in cultivating the ground, I ſee no room to doubt, that in the courſe of a few years, the country will be able to yield grain enough for the ſupport of its new poſſeſſors. But to effect this, our preſent limits muſt be greatly extended, which will require detachments of troops not to be ſpared from the preſent eſtabliſhment. And admitting the poſition, the parent country will ſtill have to ſupply us for a much longer time with every other neceſſary of life. For after what we have ſeen, the idea of being ſoon able to breed cattle ſufficient for our conſumption, muſt appear chimerical and abſurd. From all which it is evident, that ſhould Great Britain neglect to ſend out regular ſupplies, the moſt fatal conſequences will enſue.

Speculators who may feel inclined to try their fortunes here, will do well to weigh what I have ſaid. If golden dreams of commerce and wealth flatter their imaginations, diſappointment will follow: the remoteneſs of ſituation, productions of the country, and want of connection with other parts of the world, juſtify me in the aſſertion. But to men of ſmall property, unambitious of trade, and wiſhing for retirement, I think the continent of New South Wales not without inducements. One of this deſcription, with letters of recommendation, and a ſufficient capital (after having provided for his paſſage hither) to furniſh him with an aſſortment of tools for clearing land, agri-

agricultural and domeſtic purpoſes; poſ-ſeſſed alſo of a few houſhold utenſils, a cow, a few ſheep and breeding ſows, would, I am of opinion, with proper protection and encouragement, ſucceed in obtaining a comfortable livelihood, were he well aſſured before he quitted his native country, that a proviſion for him until he might be ſettled, ſhould be ſecured; and that a grant of land on his arrival would be allotted him..

That this adventurer, if of a perſevering character and competent knowledge, might in the courſe of ten years bring matters into ſuch a train as to render himſelf comfortable and independent, I think highly probable. The ſuperfluities of his farm would enable him to purchaſe European commodities from the maſters of ſhips, which will arrive on Government account, ſufficient to ſupply his wants. But beyond this he ought not to reckon, for admitting that he might meet with ſucceſs in raiſing tobacco, rice, indigo, or vineyards (for which laſt I think the ſoil and climate admirably adopted), the diſtance

 of

of a mart to vend them at, would make the expence of tranſportation ſo exceſſive, as to cut off all hopes of a reaſonable profit; nor can there be conſumers enough here to take them off his hands, for ſo great a length of time to come, as I ſhall not be at the trouble of computing.

Should then any one, induced by this account emigrate hither, let him, before he quits England, provide all his wearing apparel for himſelf, family, and ſervants; his furniture, tools of every kind, and implements of huſbandry (among which a plough need not be included, as we make uſe of the hoe) for he will touch at no place where they can be purchaſed to advantage. If his ſheep and hogs are Engliſh alſo, it will be better. For wines, ſpirits, tobacco, ſugar, coffee, tea, rice, poultry, and many other articles, he may venture to rely on at Teneriffe or Madeira, the Brazils and Cape of Good Hope. It will not be his intereſt to draw bills on his voyage out, as the exchange of money will be found invariably againſt him, and a large diſcount alſo deducted. Drafts on the place

he

he is to touch at, or caſh (dollars if poſſible) will beſt anſwer his end.

To men of deſperate fortune and the loweſt claſſes of the people, unleſs they can procure a paſſage as indented ſervants, ſimilar to the cuſtom practiſed of emigrating to America, this part of the world offers no temptation: for it can hardly be ſuppoſed, that Government will be fond of maintaining them here until they can be ſettled, and without ſuch ſupport they muſt ſtarve.

Of the Governor's inſtructions and intentions relative to the diſpoſal of the convicts, when the term of their tranſportation ſhall be expired, I am ignorant. They will then be free men, and at liberty, I apprehend, either to ſettle in the country, or to return to Europe. The former will be attended with ſome public expence; and the latter, except in particular caſes, will be difficult to accompliſh, from the numberleſs cauſes which prevent a frequent communication between England and this continent.

A LIST

A LIST *of the Civil and Military Eſtabliſh-ments in* NEW SOUTH WALES.

Governor and Commander in Chief,
His Excellency ARTHUR PHILLIP, Eſq.

Lieutenant Governor, Robert Roſs, Eſq.

Judge of the Admiralty Court, Robert Roſs, Eſq.

Chaplain of the Settlement, the Rev. Richard Johnſon.

Judge Advocate of the Settlement, David Collins, Eſq.

Secretary to the Governor, David Collins, Eſq.

Surveyor General, Auguſtus Alt, Eſq.

Commiſſary of Stores and Proviſions, Andrew Miller, Eſq.

Aſſiſtant Commiſſary, Mr. Zechariah Clarke.

Provoſt Martial, who acts as Sheriff of Cumberland County, Mr. Henry Brewer.

Peace Officer, Mr. James Smith.

MILI-

Military Establishment.

His Majeſty's ſhip Sirius, John Hunter, Eſq. Commander.

Lieutenants, —— Bradley, King, Maxwell.

His Majeſty's armed Brig, Supply, Lieutenant Henry Lidgbird Ball, Commander.

Four Companies of Marines.

Major Robert Ross, Commandant.

Captains commanding Companies,

James Campbell, John Shea,
Captain Lieutenants, James Meredith,
Watkin Tench.

Firſt Lieutenants.

George Johnſon,	John Johnſon,
John Creſwell,	James Maitland Shairp,
Robert Nellow,	Thomas Davey,
James Furzer,	Thomas Timins,
John Poulden,	

Second Lieutenants.

Ralph Clarke,	John Long,
William Dawes,	William Feddy.

U

Adiu-

Adjutant, John Long.

Quarter Maſter, James Furzer.

Aid de Camp to the Governor, George Johnſon.

Officer of Engineers and Artillery, William Dawes.

HOSPITAL ESTABLISHMENT.

Surgeon General of the Settlement, John White, Eſq.

Firſt Aſſiſtant, Mr. Dennis Conſiden.

Second Aſſiſtant, Mr. Thomas Arndell.

Third Aſſiſtant, Mr. William Balmain.

FINIS.

www.ingramcontent.com/pod-product-compliance
Ingram Content Group UK Ltd.
Pitfield, Milton Keynes, MK11 3LW, UK
UKHW042152280225
455719UK00001B/288

9 781108 061681